Smart Real Estate Deals in the Bank Bailout Era and Beyond

Smart Real Estate Deals in the Bank Bailout Era and Beyond

Charles McKay

authorHOUSE®

AuthorHouse™
1663 Liberty Drive
Bloomington, IN 47403
www.authorhouse.com
Phone: 1-800-839-8640

© *2010 Charles McKay. All rights reserved.*

No part of this book may be reproduced, stored in a retrieval system, or transmitted by any means without the written permission of the author.

First published by AuthorHouse   1/27/2010

ISBN: 978-1-4490-7724-2 (e)
ISBN: 978-1-4490-7723-5 (sc)
ISBN: 978-1-4490-7722-8 (hc)

Library of Congress Control Number: 2010900769

Printed in the United States of America
Bloomington, Indiana

This book is printed on acid-free paper.

Smart Real Estate Deals in the Bank Bailout Era and Beyond

Who Is This Book For?	xi
How This Book Is Organized	xii
Companion Web Site	xiv
Sample Files	xv
Acknowledgements	xvii
About the Author	xix

Part 1— Real Estate Investment Forecast Overview	1
What Can You Afford?	1
Financing Sources	2
Property Types	5
Markets	5
Strategies	6
Mortgages	6
Real Estate Valuation Forecast Basis	7
Rental Income	7
Operational Costs	8
Tenant Improvements and Loan Costs	9
Tax Rates	9
Sales Transaction	9
Analyzing the Real Estate Deal	11
Lease Values	11
Financial Partners	11
Refinancing	13
Comparing Real Estate Deals	13
Part 2— Cutting Costs	15
Reducing Expenses and Going Green	15
Save on Your Electric Bill	16
Bidding Out Jobs to Vendors	17
Part 3— Bank Bailout Results from Improper Valuation, Negligent	
Origination, and Exuberance	19
The Bank Bailout	19
Mortgage Origination Standard Process	20
Loan Approvals Take into Account Three Main Steps	20
Refinancing or Getting a Brand-New Loan	21

Irrational Exuberance Applied to Real Estate	22
Commercial Mortgage-backed Securities	25
Before the Bailout	25
Why Banks Received Bailout Money	28
Failed Banks	29
The Bailout Banks	31
New Strategies on Real Estate Investments in the Bailout Era	42
New Financial Deals in Commercial Real Estate	42
How Financing Has Changed in Commercial Real Estate since the Bank Bailout	43
Investment Options in Real Estate	47
Tax Credits	48
New Purchase Options	49
Commercial Brokerage Thoughts on Bailout Process	49
Private Equity Post-bailout	50
My Real Estate Portfolio Is Not Performing, Now What?	50
Bank Bailout Impact	50
Part 4— In Trouble with Your Mortgage	**55**
Foreclosure versus Short Sale	55
Credit Score Issue	55
Credit History	56
Current Employment	56
Future Employment	56
Deficiency Judgment	56
Deficiency Amount	57
Part 5— Going Pro as a Real Estate Professional	**59**
Real Estate Sales Best Practices	59
Positions in Portfolio Management	60
Real Estate Portfolio Investment Objectives	61
Part 6— Smart Real Estate Deals	**63**
Tutorial Overview of Leverage for Real Estate Investment	63
Mortgage Financing	66
Rent projections	67
Expenses (Individual)	69
Expenses (Overall)	70
Property Setup and Configuration	71

Financial Review	71
Report Output	72
Lease Value	73
Deal Value	74
Evaluate Deal—Net Present Value (NPV)	75
Property Valuation	76
Sell Property—Value at Future date.	78
Compare mortgages	78
Refinancing	79
Customer Support	80
Getting Started: Real Estate Forecast—Leverage	82

Real Estate for Sale

The Capitol in Washington, DC

Who Is This Book For?

This book is for homeowners, investors, real estate professionals, lenders, accountants, historians, and bailout banks. Homeowners benefit by finding out how much more money they can save over what they are retaining today. Real estate professionals can use this book to re-service their customers and provide new value-added services. After getting into trouble with non-performing loans, lenders can use techniques discussed in the later chapters to more accurately determine real estate values. Of course, lenders want to obtain as much cash flow as possible, but since those desires backfired in 2008–09, I would suspect that many lenders would want another method to verify the actual worth of the amount that they are loaning out. In addition, lenders can use techniques in this book to win over the confidence of potential real estate customers. Accountants can use the techniques used in the chapters to verify the investment assumptions that their customers have, compare investment approaches, and make recommendations to their customers about investing and selling decisions in real estate. Bailout banks can use methods discussed here as another way of assessing what they are loaning out.

Historians may find that this book represents the era where United States citizens need to get the most out of their money. At the time of writing this book, November 2009, the United States unemployment rate is over 10 percent, the highest rate since the Great Depression of the 1930s. Just two years ago, gasoline prices were over four dollars per gallon, the highest it has ever been, draining money from Americans who spend a significant amount of time commuting in their automobiles. Saving money in energy and becoming less dependent on oil as an energy resource has become one of the main agendas of President Obama's administration. Health care reform cost has become another major issue in President Obama's administration. Many banks have either shut down or merged with other banks. Indeed, controlling the cost for goods, services, and property is critical in this era.

How This Book Is Organized

The first section of this book gives an overview of real estate investment forecasting. It starts by discussing what a person can realistically afford when purchasing property and is followed by discussing various sources of money for your down payment beyond what most people traditionally use. The subsequent segment touches upon property types, markets, and strategies in real estate investing. An overview of sales transactions, comparing deals, and saving money from refinancing follows. I follow up by discussing the benefit of including partners in your investing, comparing real estate deals with methods of buying real estate, and valuing simple leases. Selling the property, the assumptions in determining the worth, and the derived real estate value as a result of the sale conclude this section. Determining if the property is with the broker's listing price assuming the bank loan terms is covered in later chapters.

Part 2 of the book discusses non-traditional methods to save money and cut costs. The goal is to increase cash flow. The sections are primarily for the smartest investors who want to save as much as possible in operating as real estate investors. Green and cleaner energy is discussed for investors willing to make upgrades to their investment properties. A conversation on cutting costs in utilities and with vendors ends this section.

Part 3 of this book discusses the bank bailout. I begin by discussing the process for vetting a borrower. This is followed up by discussing the state of the loan market competition during that period. Next, I discuss the practices that led up to real estate exuberance. The TARP and the related financial institutions provide supporting evidence for what actually happened. The situation sets the stage for the new direction needed in the market. I follow up by talking about the new trends in financing real estate and new real estate–related investment vehicles. Private equity options and the bank bailout impact wrap up this section.

Part 4 discusses options if you're in trouble with your mortgage. You may be facing a foreclosure. I present alternative options for you or anyone you know who is facing this dilemma.

Part 5 is for those that want to focus on real estate as a profession. I discuss tactics for selling real estate for every professional as well as the objectives of commonly held positions of personnel at real estate investment firms.

Part 6 covers a software program that I invented called Leverage for Real Estate, an investment forecasting package sold by Glacier Concept. The software allows the user to value a property in less than a half hour where it would take an appraiser a couple of days. There's a section on how to get started quickly and a full tutorial on the "Leverage for Real Estate" software. I converse about modeling your real estate deal's worth. I discuss how to finance, how to price expected average income, and common expenses. This is followed by how to account for other expenses involved in purchasing the property and how to manage the cost of improving the property to put it in order for new tenants. The software is great for beginners and is as easy to use as a video game.

Companion Web Site

Additional notes will be posted on the Glacier Concept Web site (*www.glacierconcept.com*). Notices about upgrades to the real estate forecasting software called "Leverage Personal Edition for Real Estate" will also be posted on the Glacier Concept Web site.

Sample Files

Files that can be loaded to test are available from the Glacier Concept Web site (*www.glacierconcept.com*). These files can be used for scenario comparison analysis and for the reader to learn. The data in the files are relevant to the financial models used and built to discuss what's going on in the Web site.

Acknowledgements

I acknowledge the time and support of Constance Perrier, Steve Gable, Sebastian Morel, and Eagleson Ho, who worked with me when I was creating financial and testing models. I'd like to thank David Jennings, Andrew Frazier, Sae-Wai Lee, Waldo Best, Gene Robbins, John Grooms, Vicki Grooms, Brian Reid, Richard Bonsall, Lee Smith, and Wendell Hanes for encouraging me to pursue this endeavor.

I appreciate the consistent support of my mom, Ruth, and my late dad, Charles, who always told me to pursue my dreams.

I'm pleased about the support and encouragement of Chestnut Hill Academy, Massachusetts Institute of Technology, Brown University, and their alumni, who have always been generous with their time, knowledge, and resources in my entrepreneurial pursuits. I would like to thank God and Jesus.

About the Author

My involvement in real estate valuation and asset management started when I managed revenues, operational expenses, and cash flow reporting and created amounts distributed to investors and reports for private equity firms and the firms' investors in commercial real estate in the Boston, Massachusetts, area. These investors range from wealthy individuals to publicly traded companies. I created an asset management software model to facilitate these tasks for the chairmen and chief executives. In the next year, I created simple valuation techniques after I met with other alumnae from M.I.T. (Massachusetts Institute of Technology) who, like me, believed that forecasting was the next step. The forecasting software models expanded to more complex methods of valuation in conjunction with a boutique real estate investment banks during the merger and acquisition process in commercial and residential real estate. Next, I enhanced financial models used by particular insurance companies and investment banks in verifying the worth of real estate when a new borrower engaged them in the buying process before the loan was made. This was followed by working with private equity firms to value debt on real estate. Prior to working in real estate, I re-engineered business processes for banks and insurance companies to save them millions of dollars and created new processes that have made some financial institutions millions of dollars. What an experience in financial services after receiving a degree from M.I.T. and a graduate degree from Brown University!

Part One:
Real Estate Investment Forecast Overview

What Can You Afford?

A household can typically afford a home that's approximately one-third of their gross annual income. Buying and keeping a good house typically means keeping your debt low and spending wisely. So who rents today? Mainly people who have not been educated about real estate, who live transient lives, who do not think that they can afford a home, who have not tried to get a loan, or who are waiting to get married to purchase a house.

So let's address the question of renting or buying. First of all, renters can move relatively easily and do not have to cover the cost of maintenance and repairs. There are no tax benefits unless you have a home office. The downside is that as a renter you can become evicted. Money and job stability becomes tough during an economic downturn. In addition, if the landlord decides to raise the rent, renters have no control, outside of finding a new place to live. Finding another place may not be a bad option if you have a bad landlord. There's no equity gained whatsoever in renting, and typically, the money is thrown away.

Real estate buyers are in quite a different situation. First, there's a sense of community and stability in a neighborhood. Buyers can change the landscape on the property, and financial equity is gained. The drawbacks are property taxes, and you can be foreclosed on and lose equity in the investment. Having maintenance and repairs comes with buying real estate. Buyers typically do not live a mobile lifestyle and cannot move across country easily.

Financing Sources

Real estate can be financed in both traditional and non-traditional ways. Most people typically think of getting a bank loan from an advertisement such as dialing the phone number that they see or hear on commercials to get the money for their property. Many other ways are possible. Family and friends can provide the down payment on the property that you're looking to buy. The advantage is that they may not ask for the money back as quickly. Family and friends may not ask you for interest on the amount borrowed.

Promissory notes are another option for financing your real estate purchase. A note is a legal document stating that you borrowed money from an individual and stating the terms on which you'll pay back the money. Wealthy individuals are candidates to ask for and obtain promissory notes. They may have the money, and their terms of repayment may not be as strict as the standard institutional lender.

When seeking financing from more traditional types of lenders, credit unions offer fair terms. In order to borrow from a credit union, you must first become a member of that credit union. Nearly all credit unions are connected with a significantly sized company from which the credit union developed. If you work for the company that's affiliated with the credit union, then your real estate payments can come directly from your paycheck. Getting references and verifying employment from a reputable place that's affiliated with the credit union facilitates the loan process. Credit unions may make exceptions if your credit report has flaws because they have the ability to deduct the mortgage payment directly from your paycheck and to sweep an amount into a credit union checking account.

Mortgage brokers are an entirely different option. Mortgage brokers are paid approximately 1 percent to 2 percent of your loan. Brokers may also get higher commissions based on the loan type, and they work typically on a commission-only pay basis. This means that they have an incentive to make the most money possible from every person to whom they sell a loan. A mortgage broker may also work harder to find as many options possible to get a loan on your behalf from their lenders.

Banks provide an alternative financing solution with guidelines that are stricter. Many do not make exceptions for a few mistakes in your credit report. Unless you've worked with a branch manager in the past in other social groups, there's hardly any flexibility in giving loans outside of the bank's criteria. Credit reports, tax returns, and job verifications are the main items checked. On occasion, there may be a job or personal reference.

Private equity firms provide an entirely different arrangement for financing real estate. Private equity is used for larger residential projects and commercial real estate projects.

Property Types

The number of suites, square footage, land, and property types should be the first consideration when evaluating real estate. Industrial, residential, hotels, office, shopping centers, government, multi-family, retail, and mixed-use space require different expertise to ensure property performance. Industrial property is your typical warehouses, manufacturing plants, seaports, and airports. Residential real estate is property where people live. Office space is classified as being where office parks and non-retail business property exists. Shopping centers are your typical malls. Mixed-use real estate contains a combination of more than one property type.

Markets

Location and geography play a major role in the success of a property. In 2008–2009, foreclosed property and mortgage real estate toxic assets hurt many banks in California, Florida, Georgia, Michigan, Nevada, and Arizona. The contributing cause ranged from the local economy in these areas, the kinds of mortgages that lenders sold to new owners, and the employment rates in these states to the types of businesses in the area.

Charles McKay

Strategies

Whether a person decides to pursue office space, retail, residential, shopping centers, mixed use, residential rental, or skyscrapers as a type of property, each has its distinct advantage and market. Office space properties typically have multi-year leases.

Retail properties can be lucrative in the right location because you can charge the customer a large amount per square foot for rent based on location. Retail space can vary depending on the building class and path of customer entry. In making the property attractive, the selection of tenants should be determined by how you want your property to be viewed. However, a tenant that is willing and able to pay the rent is significant despite the industry that the tenant serves.

Mortgages

Mortgages come in all kinds of flavors, but the ones for residential and commercial real estate that you should be most familiar with are normal mortgages and balloon mortgages. Each has advantages to the issuer and perhaps to the borrower. Typically, the borrower does not think about the principal and the interest separately before applying for a loan. Most often, the main concern of the borrower is whether the lender will allow them to borrow the amount asked for and whether there's a definitive plan to pay the money back.

Real Estate Valuation Forecast Basis

The property type, whether commercial or residential, will give the buyer financial tax advantages when determining cash flow. You should determine the amount that you want to charge for rent and the rent calculation methods when buying property. The amount of square footage is directly tied to the amount of monthly rent if a person is being charged on a per-square-foot basis. Develop a great name for the real estate project.

Rental Income

The basis of rent may vary from gross value to a per-square-foot basis. Per-square-foot metrics are typically used to measure against a market basis. Other costs may be measured on this basis as well. A gross value helps most residential customers understand the pricing. Residents are mainly concerned with how much the rent is per month. When creating a projection on a multi-tenant property, consider the number of units and the average monthly cost and basis for the rent per unit.

Charles McKay

Operational Costs

Both commercial and residential properties have costs associated with someone managing the property. If this expense is outsourced, it ranges typically from 2 to 10 percent of the rent. If you are managing the property yourself, then the management fee costs nothing. Other common operational expenses are property insurance, maintenance, repairs, and property taxes. Occasionally heating, cooling, and accounting expenses may be significant depending on your market such as New England, Florida, or Texas. To maximize cash flow, it is necessary to keep expenses low.

Tenant Improvements and Loan Costs

Tenant improvements and loan costs are depreciated and amortized when forecasting. Tenant improvements are the costs associated with improving the building or tenant suite. These improvements can influence a tenant to choose to occupy one building over another in the market.

Loan costs are the other profitable fees associated with the mortgage loan that the lender passes onto the borrower. The loan costs may include the commission and operational fees that the lending officer charges for processing the loan.

Tax Rates

Combined federal and state taxes influence the cash flow from commercial and residential properties while the owner maintains the property. At the time of sale, a sales tax is applied to the cost.

Sales Transaction

The sales transaction occurs in two different parts: sales valuation and the actual transaction. Real estate negotiation and determining actual worth are pertinent in this area. Without getting a strong sense of the worth and metrics, a buyer can spend a significant amount of money over what the property is actually worth and later potentially get into trouble when contractually tied to paying the mortgage debt, unless the property is paid for in full when the sale occurs. When buying or selling a cash flow generating property, the sale valuation should be based on the actual cash flow. At times, brokers want to assign the worth based on an assumed cash flow if the property were filled with a hypothetical or market-based rate. If the property is not making as much money, then the buyer should be able to negotiate the price with the broker. If the property is one hundred percent occupied and generating money, the price should be valued at the annual amount of rent divided by the market capitalization rate. Capitalization rates will vary from market to market. The actual price will be sensitive to the assumed capitalization rate. A buyer should be really aware of market capitalization rates and get multiple assessments before agreeing to what the listing broker states is the capitalization rate. Most brokers do not mention the capitalization rate to an unsophisticated buyer and just want the buyer to pay the listed asking price.

The actual sales transaction involves subtracting the current mortgage, remaining improvements, loan costs, and taxes when determining the money made from the property sale.

Analyzing the Real Estate Deal

When analyzing the real estate deal, it is vital to understand when you'll make your money back as well as whether you need to sell the property at a future date to make a profit. Estimating when the money will be made back by the initial investment is imperative. The profitability and return rate of the projection are other crucial metrics in analyzing the deal.

Lease Values

The present value of money is determined based on the number of years, metrics, and terms of the lease. The lease is contracted revenue that the renter is obligated to pay. A lease can have an interest rate assigned. The person who signs a tenant to the lease agreement based on one or multiple years should think of the contract as the amount in today's dollars that the contract is worth.

Financial Partners

There are a number of methods to construct real estate deals and to purchase property even if you do not have all of the money yourself. Getting financial partners and splitting the profit either based on cash contribution, experience level, management of the new real estate asset, or a combination of the above are all options. In your plan, consider the before-tax and after-tax amounts that will be contributed by each individual party. It's a good strategy to get as many partners as possible to get the property that you want. If you do your first deal, you should be able to do additional deals in the future.

There are a few entity structures that exist for doing deals; there are pros and cons to each. Some of the common ones are limited liability companies, limited liability partnerships, limited partnerships, joint tenancy, tenants in common, and general partnerships. Other structures include C corporations, S corporations, and REITs (Real Estate Investment Trusts), but I will not discuss those in this book.

Limited liability companies are a hybrid of a company and a limited partnership. The owners of an LLC are members. The entity is taxed like a partnership, only once. Individual members are not responsible for the debt of the partnerships. LLCs are incredibly easy to form. The members need special documents in order to raise money. In an LLP or Limited Liability Partnership, members can take part in running the business. They are liable for the entity's debt but only up to the amount of their participation in the LLP. General partnerships have two or more members involved to run a project to or a business. General partnerships are better than owning a business on your own. However, raising money is challenging in general partnerships. Tenants in common are entities where two or more people have ownership. The ownership structure may be unequal, but general partnerships are better than individual ownership structures. A joint tenancy structure has multiple owners that share equal stakes. If an owner dies, then the remaining owners can take the diseased owner's portion.

Refinancing

Refinancing allows the owner of the property to save money if the cost of the loan and pre-payment penalties on the current loan plus the cost of the refinance do not outweigh the obligations to the current loan. The benefit of the loan refinance is to either the homeowner or property owner. The achievement is the reduction of debt and monthly expenses and increase in household cash flow. Refinancing the loan to a lower interest rate with better loan terms than the current mortgage is the best option.

Comparing Real Estate Deals

Getting the better deal depends on your strategy. Do you want the most profitable deal where you'll maximize your return rate? Do you want to pay the lowest possible cost on the property? Do you want to pay the least amount in bank fees? The best overall situation is to gain the best return rate possible while paying the lowest cost on the property. The amount of capital you have may decide your ability to negotiate bank term fees and the property cost. The last part of this book will allow the buyer to generate a forecast and optimize the return rate given different loan terms.

Part Two: Cutting Costs

Cutting costs on your energy and utility bills and vendors.

Reducing Expenses and Going Green

The easiest way to reduce costs associated with your real estate investment is to reduce your expenses and start with utilities. As for electricity, you should change your lighting. I experienced a sixty-five percent reduction in my electricity bill when I went from traditional light bulbs to florescent lights. Next, use motion detectors to control the on/off feature of lighting. They will only keep the lights on if you are actually in the room. By purchasing florescent bulbs, you can receive credits from your local electric company in most states. Next, change the insulation materials in your attic. So far, fire-resistant cellulose insulation has shown to stop air infiltration better than fiberglass. Many fire-resistant cellulose manufacturers have a heat transfer resistance (R) value of 3.6–3.8, which surpasses fiberglass at 2.6. Fire-resistant cellulose insulation has proven to save energy up to 40 percent and will also reduce your heating and cooling bills. The American Recovery and Reinvestment Act of 2009 will allow homeowners a 30 percent federal tax credit to $1500. If you can afford a new heating system, then go solar. With a solar-based system, you'll change the control systems and can sell electricity back to the electric company. Geothermal heating systems are another option that can help save money in different areas of the country. Geothermal systems use the ground to heat in-ground coils that also come into the home to provide energy. Replacing all your current water faucets with good faucet aerators can reduce your water usage up to fifty percent and lower your water bill.

Other non-traditional bills associated with cost reduction include property taxes, insurance, maintenance, repairs, landscaping, and snow removal. Try to find a dependable lower-cost provider for insurance. Shop around and bid out maintenance, repairs, landscaping, and snow removal services.

For buildings under consideration for new construction, integrated building design and sharing an energy source should be considered. Furthermore, systems design with control systems that use a hybrid of sources can reduce carbon emissions.

Save on Your Electric Bill

Get smart strips surge protectors to reduce idle energy use. Smart strips will limit the power when electric appliances are not in use. Buy spiral florescent light bulbs. Twenty-three watts replace between seventy-five and ninety watts of light, with the same relative brightness. Upgrading insulation, thermostats, doors, and windows will save you hundreds of dollars per year. For appliances, buy an energy star–qualified appliance. Air sealing foam and weather seals can eliminate drafts around windows and doors starting at $4.00.

Bidding Out Jobs to Vendors

Finding the lowest cost vendors for commodity services such as repairs, snow removal, landscaping, custodial services, and maintenance will reduce your expenses. Perform due diligence to ensure the vendor is dependable before making a switch.

Part Three: Bank Bailout Results from Improper Valuation, Negligent Origination, and Exuberance

The Bank Bailout

The bank bailout occurred as a result of a faulty economic model and incorrect asset valuations. These valued assets were sold and transferred to buyers on the expectation that the money could be repaid and the financial goals could be achieved. Only some of the problems on economic model and GDP (Gross Domestic Product), are discussed in this book. This book does not cover the reasons why some investment banks that trade hundreds of thousands and millions of dollars on margin were bailed out by the US Treasury because they did not have enough capital cash reserves to cover their bad investments when the people and companies who loaned them money wanted their cash from their margin calls. Companies received funds from the Troubled Assets Relief Program (TARP) to save them from bankruptcy. It's thought by the public that the real estate toxic assets are difficult to value. In reality, many of the real estate assets were not valued correctly when they were sold to buyers the first time around. Some mortgage loan originators sold money to buyers that did not have the capacity to pay if there was the slightest change in the economy. The asset value when combined with the mortgage type or mortgage package bound to the property can make the asset toxic as an investment vehicle. When normal and toxic assets are coiled up with one another and are sold as a security, investors and security traders have a difficult time understanding what they are really purchasing and its actual worth.

Mortgage Origination Standard Process

Once the borrower has made a decision to purchase a property and has chosen a bank, a traditional lender, or mortgage broker for the financing, there are a few standard steps. Unfortunately these steps were not followed properly. The origination process was broken during the real estate bubble and contributed to leading Wall Street to its doom.

Loan Approvals Take into Account Three Main Steps

- ❑ Credit check: The applicant's mortgage history is checked and a credit report is obtained.
- ❑ Qualification: The applicant's ability to pay is reviewed. Income statements and assets are verified. W2s, tax returns, pay stubs,

and bank statements are collected. Liabilities are determined through credit reports. Qualifying ratios are calculated.
- ❑ Property value: An appraisal is conducted on the property.

Refinancing or Getting a Brand-New Loan

Borrowers typically receive their approvals within a week. Eighteen percent to 36 percent of applicants receive their loan approvals after a week. One quarter of the applicants' loans closed within a week on average, another quarter of the applicants close within two weeks, and the remainder can take up to four weeks or more for closing. If you have not heard from the lender in over five weeks, then contact the lender because there may be a problem. The lender could have gone out of business.

What are the costs and timing for mortgage refinancing?

The application

- ❑ The cost is approximately $225.

Loan approval

- ❑ Underwriting costs are approximately $175.
- ❑ Survey's cost are approximately $125.
- ❑ Origination (the commission to the loan officer and his or company) is one point or 1 percent of the loan amount. This fee can be higher under some circumstances.
- ❑ Credit report costs $50.
- ❑ The flood certification fee is $25.

- An appraisal cost approximately $335.
- The document preparation fee is approximately $175.
- The tax service costs approximately $75.

Settlement

- The notary fee is approximately $75.
- Attorney fees are approximately $500.
- The title search costs (for insurance) are approximately $400.

What occurred during the mortgage bubble was that there were people in the business of selling loans who either stretched the truth or found alternative loan programs that failed. Loan originators pushed borrowers for the sale and told them that they could get them the money for the house and may have inflated the amount of income that the borrower actually earned.

Instead, I recommend the following approach for the buyer. Negotiate a price with the seller, either directly or through a broker. Next, determine how much money you can raise from friends and family. If you cannot obtain the amount you need from non-traditional lenders discussed earlier in the book, ask traditional lenders for the remaining amount to finance your real estate investment.

Irrational Exuberance Applied to Real Estate

During many real estate peaks and bubbles, such as 2004–2006, irrational exuberance leads to a credit crisis. Increases in competition led to lower standards of underwriting deals. Low interest rates drove financing strategies, investment decisions, and methods of operations.

When deals and the borrowers are risky and the rules of buying property changes, the loans become more risky. Lenders sold their loans to Wall Street, and they were put into tranches. Many mortgage obligations were securitized again and were converted to collateralized debt or CDOs by financial institutions. As long as mortgages of various types could be sold to Wall Street, loans were written and sold. Consequently, mortgage brokers were paid their origination fees. The competition for loan leads among competing firms led to taking on customers with poor credit, lack of due diligence, and loan fraud.

It is believed that the rating agencies have flaws in their system. Traders of securitized debt became over-optimistic. Many investors believed that the values would increase forever. Sub-primes that reset were going to face bankruptcy eventually.

If the CDOs and securitized debt do not perform, then the Wall Street investors, funds, and traders do not make their expected returns. Consequently, the funds lose their value. Holes in the housing balloon led to credit market confidence loss.

So, why do foreclosures continue? Mortgages reset, people lose jobs, and delinquencies on payments occur, defaults increase, and the foreclosure process begin. ARM re-sets are still an issue. Many firms were devastated. Basis Capital, American Home Mortgage, Bear Stearns, BNP Paribas, JER Investors, Archstone-Smith/Tishman-Speyer Properties, KKR Financial, and Countrywide Financial were among the big losers. Many of these firms had losses ranging from $40 million to $11 billion. Recently both CIT and Citigroup have been having trouble.

Can asset class diversification eliminate systematic failure? Probably not. This is why gold prices in November 2009 have risen to record levels. Gold has historically been a risk-free substance and is the basis on which many currencies are exchanged and valued.

There was demand coming out of the 2002 recession, and the lending standards were loose. People wanted to get into something new. Mortgage brokers created deals. They persuaded developers and real estate brokers to influence buyers to borrow beyond what they could afford to repay. Just because people bid up a price does not mean that the property is worth the asking price. The brokers make more money by selling the most expensive house.

There was a vicious cycle, and the goal was to drive up the valuations on real estate. Many appraisers worked with brokers to mark things up 10 to 15 percent every quarter. You had property that was sold as new construction at $100,000. Four years later, according to the appraisers, it was worth $400,000. This situation caused the problems. The valuations became invalid, and the brokers marked the prices up too much. All of those properties have mortgages against them.

Commercial Mortgage-backed Securities

What failed horribly prior to the bailout was the ability of the debt buyers to evaluate how good the debt was. Of course, there were rating systems, but they were flawed. Buyers were not able to evaluate the credit quality, loan to value, debt service, property type, lease expiration, property age, location, loan maturity, number of loans, loan size, and loan terms. Credit rating helps to determine value insofar as the borrower's willingness and ability to pay. An economic downturn can influence the risk of default. In many cases, loan default is what has occurred. Since the rating system is flawed, the value is just about worthless. The investment banks that held a large portion of these securities without the proper rating have been devastated.

Before the Bailout

I realized that assets were overpriced in 2005–2006. At that time, I developed a software application called Leverage Personal Edition. In 2008, I figured that there were additional ways to determine the value of mortgage debt relative to the prices of real estate. Realizing that a bailout might be in the future, I issued a press release prior to the idea of a bailout process in a newswire at 12:47 p.m. on September 25, 2008, from New Hampshire. It read:

Congress and the House are meeting to determine its role to aid financial institutions in the current credit crisis. The decision makers in Washington DC must find out the mortgage debt's worth. Leverage Personal Edition free trial software by Glacier Concept enables the user to go through financing scenarios to determine the value, return, and profitability of the real estate investments and mortgage debts. Anyone voting to make US Treasury capital decisions must first understand how to optimize capital, cash flow, and return rates. The technology enables users to negotiate with the lender and to conclude if the property is worth the mortgage debt. The forecasting software uses 3-D graphs and charts to make the investment as easy as a video game. "The decision makers analyze the financial risk of the debt. Next, the decision maker determines whether and when they can become profitable by investing in the mortgage, based on what the borrower can afford to pay", says Glacier Concept founder Larry McKay. Glacier Concept's founders are alumni from M.I.T. (Massachusetts Institute of Technology) and Brown University.

Individual homeowners that use Leverage Personal Edition may increase the available cash in the household, help prevent bank loan foreclosure, and save thousands of dollars by negotiating a better deal in loan costs, fees, and interest. "We took the real estate investment experience of smart investors similar to Donald Bren and Donald Trump and put it to software", says Larry McKay, the inventor. The technology can

Smart Real Estate Deals in the Bank Bailout Era and Beyond help Nevada, California, Georgia, Florida, Colorado, Ohio, and Michigan residents on foreclosure threshold.

Free Trial Download available on GlacierConcept.com

http://www.glacierconcept.com/download/leverage1yeardot.exe

Using scenarios, homeowners can compare whether financing with JP Morgan Chase, Wells Fargo, Bank of America, Fannie Mae, Freddie Mac, or Countrywide Financial will save the homeowner the most money. Loan to Value, Debt Service, property types, lease expiration, property age, location, loan maturity, the number of loans, loan size, loan terms, and credit rating are measures voters, Congress and the Representatives should become familiar with when negotiating whether to use mortgage backed securities as a bail out resolution. Leverage for Real Estate Investment Software is free and can put the Treasury in the right direction to make the correct decision on which debt to purchase, at what price, while managing the tax payer capital.

Visit *http://www.glacierconcept.com*

Contact email: support@glacierconcept.com

603-866-0237

1500A Lafayette Road #259

Portsmouth, NH 03801

Glacier Concept

Larry McKay, 603-866-0237

support@glacierconcept.com

This press release was made through Business Wire prior to the election and prior to the current administration coming into office.

The White House in Washington, DC

Why Banks Received Bailout Money

There were a few different scenarios. One of them was that as a bank, you were forced to take the money for cash reserves. The next scenario was that banks needed to get back to lending and accepted money to get back on track and focus. The last scenario is that there are banks that accept the TARP money to increase capital so that they can compete.

On the real estate and debt side, competition and greed caused overpricing and astronomical valuations. Money was loaned out by banks and other institutions. Some banks kept their loans, and some sold them to Wall Street. Some asset management firms, hedge funds, and insurance companies invested in the overvalued securitized debt securities that were supposed to perform like bonds. Money from bank customer deposits was loaned out and could not be repaid. The loan sellers and brokers received their fees and commissions for marking everything up. The commercial loan investors did not know how to value the loans that they were buying.

Failed Banks

There are approximately 210 failed banks as of November 11, 2009.

They include: First Bank of Beverly Hills; First Bank of Idaho; The Columbian Bank and Trust Company; First Priority Bank; First National Bank of Nevada; John Warner Bank; First Heritage Bank; IndyMac Bank; First Integrity Bank; ANB Financial; America West Bank; American Southern Bank; Michigan Heritage Bank; Waterford Village Bank; Pinnacle Bank; FirstBank Financial Services; Alliance Bank; County Bank; MagnetBank; Freedom Bank; Riverview Community Bank; Bank of Elmwood; Flagship National Bank; Hillcrest Bank Florida; American United Bank; Irwin Union Bank; Peoples Community Bank; Integrity Bank; American Sterling Bank; Community First Bank; Community National Bank of Sarasota County; First State Bank; Alpha Bank & Trust; Main Street Bank; Meridian Bank; Washington Mutual Bank; Ameribank; Silver State Bank; Security Bank of North Fulton; First DuPage Bank; 1st Centennial Bank; National Bank of

Charles McKay

Commerce; Colorado National Bank; Teambank; Freedom Bank of Georgia; Bank of Clark County; Haven Trust Bank; Sanderson State Bank; First Georgia Community Bank; First Coweta Bank; ebank; Community Bank of Nevada; Community Bank of Arizona; Union Bank; Colonial Bank; Dwelling House Savings and Loan Association; Cape Fear Bank; Guaranty Bank; Westsound Bank; Silverton Bank; National Association; The Community Bank; Downey Savings and Loan Association; PFF Bank and Trust; Franklin Bank; CapitalSouth Bank; New Frontier Bank; Omni National Bank; FirstCity Bank; Citizens Community Bank; Security Pacific Bank; Jennings State Bank; Warren Bank; Georgian Bank; Vantus Bank; InBank; First Bank of Kansas City; Affinity Bank; Mainstreet Bank; Bradford Bank; Suburban Federal Savings Bank; Community Bank of West Georgia; Neighborhood Community Bank; Horizon Bank; Metro Pacific Bank; Corn Belt Bank and Trust Colo.; Douglass National Bank; San Joaquin Bank; Integrity Bank; First State Bank of Altus; Security Bank of Bibb County; Irwin Union Bank and Trust Co.; Venture Bank; Brickwell Community Bank; Corus Bank, N.A.; Mirae Bank; First National Bank of Anthony; Cooperative Bank; Southern Community Bank; Great Basin Bank of Nevada; Security Bank of Houston County; Security Bank of Jones County; Security Bank of Gwinnett County; Security Bank of North Metro; Southern Colorado National Bank; Heritage Community Bank; Security Savings Bank; Silver Falls Bank; Sherman County Bank; Riverside Bank of the Gulf Coast; First State Bank; Platinum Community Bank; Partners Bank; First Piedmont Bank;

BankFirst; Vineyard Bank; Temecula Valley Bank; Bank of Wyoming; Founders Bank; Millennium State Bank of Texas; First National Bank of Danville; Elizabeth State Bank; Rock River Bank; First State Bank of Winchester; Bank of Lincolnwood; Strategic Capital Bank; Citizens National Bank; BankUnited FSB; Mutual Bank; First Bankamericano; Ocala National Bank; and Hume Bank.

This cost the FDIC approximately $40,000,000,000 (forty billion dollars). If money is loaned out from depositors' money cannot be paid back, then banks fail.

The Bailout Banks

There were numerous companies that received money from the TARP through October 2009. Approximately 683 banks accepted bailout money as of November 11, 2009.

They include: Wells Fargo & Co.; State Street Corp.; Bank of America Corp.; JPMorgan Chase & Co.; Citigroup, Inc.; Morgan Stanley; Goldman Sachs Group, Inc.; Bank of New York Mellon Corp.; Regions Financial Corp.; UCBH Holdings, Inc.; Bank of Commerce Holdings; Broadway Financial Corp.; SunTrust Banks Inc.; Northern Trust Corp.; Provident Bancshares Corp.; U.S. Bancorp; TCF Financial Corp.; BB&T Corp.; 1st FS Corp.; Valley National Bancorp; KeyCorp; Huntington Bancshares; Umpqua Holdings Corp.; First Horizon National Corp.; Comerica, Inc.; Zions Bancorporation; Capital One Financial Corp.; Washington Federal, Inc.; Marshall & Ilsley Corp.; City National

Corporation; Pacific Capital Bancorp; Heritage Commerce Corp.; First PacTrust Bancorp, Inc.; Nara Bancorp, Inc.; Webster Financial Corporation; Centerstate Banks of Florida, Inc.; Ameris Bancorp; Taylor Capital Group; Porter Bancorp, Inc.; Boston Private Financial Holdings, Inc.; Severn Bancorp, Inc.; Trustmark Corporation; First Niagara Financial Group; Western Alliance Bancorporation; First Community Corporation; HF Financial Corp.; First Community Bankshares, Inc.; Banner Corporation; Cascade Financial Corporation; Columbia Banking System, Inc.; Heritage Financial Corporation; Associated Banc-Corp; Superior Bancorp, Inc.; Manhattan Bancorp; East West Bancorp; Cathay General Bancorp; CVB Financial Corp; Bank of Marin Bancorp; Oak Valley Bancorp; Coastal Banking Company, Inc.; TIB Financial Corp; FPB Bancorp, Inc.; United Community Banks, Inc.; MB Financial, Inc.; First Midwest Bancorp, Inc.; Old National Bancorp; Blue Valley Ban Corp; Iberiabank Corporation; Central Bancorp, Inc.; Eagle Bancorp, Inc.; Sandy Spring Bancorp, Inc.; Old Line Bancshares, Inc.; Great Southern Bancorp; Southern Missouri Bancorp, Inc.; Southern Community Financial Corp.; Bank of North Carolina; Unity Bancorp, Inc.; State Bancorp, Inc.; First Defiance Financial Corp.; Central Federal Corporation; Southwest Bancorp, Inc.; Popular, Inc.; South Financial Group, Inc.; First Financial Holdings, Inc.; Encore Bancshares, Inc.; Wesbanco Bank, Inc.; Sterling Financial Corporation; Bank of the Ozarks, Inc.; SVB Financial Group; Center Financial Corp.; Wilshire Bancorp, Inc.; First Litchfield Financial Corp.; Wilmington Trust Corp.; The Bancorp, Inc.; Indiana Community

Bancorp; HopFed Bancorp; LSB Corp.; Northeast Bancorp; Citizens Republic Bancorp, Inc.; Independent Bank Corp.; Capital Bank Corp.; NewBridge Bancorp; Citizens South Banking Corp.; Signature Bank; LNB Bancorp, Inc.; Susquehanna Bancshares, Inc.; National Penn Bancshares, Inc.; Fidelity Bancorp, Inc.; Pinnacle Financial Partners, Inc.; Sterling Bancshares, Inc.; TowneBank; Valley Financial Corp.; Virginia Commerce Bancorp; Pacific International Bancorp; BancTrust Financial Group, Inc.; Community; West Bancshares; Summit State Bank; Santa Lucia Bancorp; First California Financial Group, Inc; Pacific City Financial Corporation; Exchange Bank; NCAL Bancorp; CoBiz Financial, Inc.; The Connecticut Bank and Trust Company; Seacoast Banking Corporation of Florida; Synovus Financial Corp.; Fidelity Southern Corporation; Heartland Financial USA, Inc.; Intermountain Community Bancorp; Wintrust Financial Corporation; Marquette National Corporation; Bridgeview Bancorp, Inc.; Horizon Bancorp; FFW Corporation; Fidelity Financial Corporation; Citizens First Corporation; FCB Bancorp, Inc.; Whitney Holding Corporation; Wainwright Bank & Trust Company; Berkshire Hills Bancorp, Inc.; OneUnited Bank; Tri-County Financial Corporation; Patapsco Bancorp, Inc.; Enterprise Financial Services Corp.; Hawthorn Bancshares, Inc.; Monadnock Bancorp, Inc.; Flushing Financial Corporation; The Elmira Savings Bank, FSB; Alliance Financial Corporation; Mid Penn Bancorp, Inc.; VIST Financial Corp.; AmeriServ Financial, Inc; Bancorp Rhode Island, Inc.; Security Federal Corporation; Tidelands Bancshares, Inc; Tennessee Commerce Bancorp, Inc.; Plains Capital Corporation; Patriot

Bancshares, Inc.; Community Bankers Trust Corporation; Community Financial Corporation; Monarch Financial Holdings, Inc.; StellarOne Corporation; Union Bankshares Corporation; SunTrust Banks, Inc.; West Bancorporation, Inc.; First Banks, Inc.; CIT Group, Inc.; Fifth Third Bancorp; The PNC Financial Services Group, Inc.; Hampton Roads Bankshares, Inc.; Commerce National Bank; Security California Bancorp; Security Business Bancorp; Mission Community Bancorp; Valley Community Bank; Colony Bankcorp, Inc.; The Queensborough Company; Central Pacific Financial Corp.; North Central Bancshares, Inc.; American State Bancshares, Inc.; Farmers Capital Bank Corporation; First Financial Service Corporation; MidSouth Bancorp, Inc.; Community Trust Financial Corporation; Independent Bank Corp.; Shore Bancshares, Inc.; Rising Sun Bancorp; The First Bancorp, Inc.; Redwood Financial, Inc.; Centrue Financial Corporation; Cadence Financial Corporation; Bank of America Corp.; Crescent Financial Corporation; Carolina Bank Holdings, Inc.; First Bancorp; Sound Banking Company; Surrey Bancorp; Peapack-Gladstone Financial Corporation;

Sun Bancorp, Inc.; Center Bancorp, Inc.; American Express Company; New York Private Bank & Trust Corporation; FirstMerit Corporation; LCNB Corp.; F.N.B. Corporation; Codorus Valley Bancorp, Inc.; Independence Bank; GrandSouth Bancorporation; Congaree Bancshares, Inc.; First Security Group, Inc.; Texas National Bancorporation; Eastern Virginia Bankshares, Inc.; C&F Financial Corporation; Home Bancshares, Inc.; Southern Bancorp, Inc.;

Community 1st Bank; Pacific Coast National Bancorp; Community Bank of the Bay; Redwood Capital Bancorp; Syringa Bancorp; Idaho Bancorp; Old Second Bancorp, Inc.; First Bankers Trustshares, Inc.; MainSource Financial Group, Inc.; Morrill Bancshares, Inc.; Bar Harbor Bankshares (Bar Harbor Bank & Trust); United Bancorp, Inc.; Pulaski Financial Corp Creve; Dickinson Financial Corporation II; ECB Bancorp, Inc.(East Carolina Bank); Yadkin Valley Financial Corporation; Bank of Commerce; State Bankshares, Inc.; BNCCORP, Inc.; New Hampshire Thrift Bancshares, Inc.; Somerset Hills Bancorp; OceanFirst Financial Corp.; Carver Bancorp, Inc; S&T Bancorp; Citizens & Northern Corporation; First BanCorp; SCBT Financial Corporation; Texas Capital Bancshares, Inc.; MetroCorp Bancshares. Inc.; TCB Holding Company (Texas Community Bank); Treaty Oak Bancorp, Inc.; United Financial Banking Companies, Inc.; Centra Financial Holdings, Inc.(Centra Bank, Inc.); Washington Banking Company (Whidbey Island Bank); Puget Sound Bank; The Baraboo Bancorporation; First Manitowoc Bancorp, Inc.; Liberty Bancshares, Inc.; Commonwealth Business Bank; CalWest Bancorp; Fresno First Bank; First ULB Corp.; California Oaks State Bank; WSFS Financial Corporation; Seaside National Bank & Trust; Alarion Financial Services, Inc.; Princeton National Bancorp, Inc.; Midland States Bancorp, Inc.; Southern Illinois Bancorp, Inc.; 1st Source Corporation; FPB Financial Corp.; Crosstown Holding Company; BankFirst Capital Corporation; Calvert Financial Corporation; AB&T Financial Corporation; First Citizens Banc Corp; Stonebridge Financial Corp.; Moscow Bancshares,

Charles McKay

Inc.; Farmers Bank; Pierce County Bancorp; Goldwater Bank; Rogers Bancshares, Inc.; Peninsula Bank Holding Co.; Central Valley Community Bancorp; Plumas Bancorp; Valley Commerce Bancorp; Ojai Community Bank; Beach Business Bank; Bankers' Bank of West Bancorp, Inc.; First Southern Bancorp, Inc.; Metro City Bank; Private Bancorp, Inc.; AMB Financial Corp.; UBT Bancshares, Inc.; Equity Bancshares, Inc.; Katahdin Bankshares Corp.; First United Corporation; Annapolis Bancorp, Inc.; Monument Bank; Flagstar Bancorp, Inc.; Firstbank Corporation; Guaranty Federal Bancshares, Inc.; Oak Ridge Financial Services, Inc.; Nortdway Financial, Inc.; Parke Bancorp, Inc.; Stewardship Financial Corporation; Community Partners Bancorp; Hilltop Community Bancorp, Inc.;

Adbanc, Inc; Country Bank Shares, Inc.; Peoples Bancorp, Inc.; DNB Financial Corporation; First Resource Bank; Greer Bancshares Incorporated; F & M Bancshares, Inc.; Central Bancshares, Inc.; Central Virginia Bankshares, Inc.; Middleburg Financial Corporation; WashingtonFirst Bank; W.T.B. Financial Corporation; Anchor BanCorp Wisconsin, Inc.; Legacy Bancorp, Inc.; Alaska Pacific Bancshares, Inc.; US Metro Bank; First Western Financial, Inc.; Community Holding Company of Florida, Inc.; Georgia Commerce Bancshares, Inc.; PGB Holdings, Inc.; MidWestOne Financial Group, Inc.; The Freeport State Bank.; Citizens Commerce Bancshares, Inc.; Todd Bancshares, Inc.; Liberty Financial Services, Inc.; Mercantile Capital Corp.; Monarch Community Bancorp, Inc.; The First Bancshares, Inc.; Carolina Trust Bank; F & M Financial Corporation; The Bank of Currituck; Centrix

Bank & Trust; Lakeland Bancorp, Inc.; Pascack Community Bank; First Express of Nebraska, Inc.; Banner County Ban Corporation; Hyperion Bank; Stockmens Financial Corporation; CedarStone Bank; Lone Star Bank; First Market Bank, FSB; First Bank of Charleston, Inc.; Corning Savings and Loan Association; Westamerica Bancorporation; 1st Enterprise Bank; Santa Clara Valley Bank, N.A.; First Choice Bank; ColoEast Bankshares, Inc.; QCR Holdings, Inc.; Bern Bancshares, Inc.; The Bank of Kentucky Financial Corporation; Hometown Bancshares, Inc.; Carrollton Bancorp; State Capital Corporation; DeSoto County Bank; Security Bancshares of Pulaski County, Inc.; Reliance Bancshares, Inc.; Gregg Bancshares, Inc.; Midwest Regional Bancorp, Inc.; Liberty Bancshares, Inc.; FNB United Corp.; PremierWest Bancorp; Meridian Bank; BankGreenville; Regional Bankshares, Inc.; F&M Financial Corp.; Peoples Bancorp; Northwest Bancorporation, Inc.; Northwest Commercial Bank; First Menasha Bancshares, Inc.; Financial Security Corporation; Hometown Bancorp of Alabama, Inc.; White River Bancshares Company; Sonoma Valley Bancorp; The Private Bank of California; United American Bank;

Premier Service Bank; Florida Business BancGroup, Inc.; Liberty Shares, Inc.; CBB Bancorp; Hamilton State Bancshares, Inc.; Northern States Financial Corporation; First BancTrust Corporation; First Merchants Corporation; Market Bancorporation, Inc.; Lafayette Bancorp, Inc.; BancPlus Corporation; Security State Bancshares, Inc.; Guaranty Bancorp, Inc.; Royal Bancshares of Pennsylvania, Inc.; First Priority Financial Corp.; Central Community Corporation; Mid-

Charles McKay

Wisconsin Financial Services, Inc.; California Bank of Commerce; Community Business Bank West; FNB Bancorp South; Columbine Capital Corp.; BNC Financial Group, Inc.; Midtown Bank & Trust Company; D.L. Evans Bancorp; Lakeland Financial Corporation; Integra Bank Corporation; Lakeland Financial Corporation; National Bancshares, Inc.; Green Circle Investments, Inc.; PSB Financial Corporation; Howard Bancorp, Inc.; First M&F Corporation; Green City Bancshares, Inc.; Catskill Hudson Bancorp, Inc; First Gothenburg Bancshares; Regent Capital Corporation; TriState Capital Holdings, Inc.; The Victory Bank; Southern First Bancshares; Community First, Inc.; Avenue Financial Holdings; Central Bancorp; First State Bank of Mobeetie; Medallion Bank; Ridgestone Financial Services; First Federal Bancshares of Arkansas, Inc.; ICB Financial; First Southwest Bancorporation, Inc.; Highlands Independent Bancshares; Pinnacle Bank Holding Company, Inc.; Marine Bank & Trust Company; Regent Bancorp, Inc.; Citizens Bancshares Corporation; PeoplesSouth Bancshares, Inc.; First Busey Corporation; Blue River Bancshares, Inc.; Community Bancshares of Kansas, Inc.; Blue Ridge Bancshares, Inc.; AmeriBank Holding Company; HCSB Financial Corporation; First Reliance Bancshares, Inc; Merchants and Planters Bancshares, Inc.; Germantown Capital Corporation, Inc.; First Texas BHC, Inc.; Farmers & Merchants Bancshares, Inc.; BOH Holdings, Inc.; Park Bancorporation, Inc.; BancIndependent, Inc.; First Northern Community Bancorp; Salisbury Bancorp, Inc.; 1st United Bancorp, Inc.; First Intercontinental Bank; Discover Financial Services; Butler

Point, Inc.; Haviland Bancshares, Inc.; Madison Financial Corporation; St. Johns Bancshares, Inc.; First American International Corp.; IBW Financial Corporation; Bank of George; First Place Financial Corp.; Provident Community Bancshares, Inc.; Moneytree Corporation; Sovereign Bancshares, Inc.; First National Corporation; Blackhawk Bancorp, Inc.; Heritage Oaks Bancorp; Premier Bank Holding Company; Farmers & Merchants Financial Corporation; Farmers State Bankshares, Inc.; First NBC Bank Holding Company; Citizens Bank & Trust Company; Kirksville Bancorp, Inc.; First Colebrook Bancorp, Inc.; Community First Bancshares, Inc.; Peoples Bancshares of TN, Inc.; SBT Bancorp, Inc.; CSRA Bank Corp.; Trinity Capital Corporation; Clover Community Bankshares, Inc.; Pathway Bancorp; Colonial American Bank West; MS Financial, Inc.; Triad Bancorp, Inc.; Alpine Banks of Colorado; Naples Bancorp, Inc.; CBS BancCorp.; IBT Bancorp, Inc.; Spirit BankCorp, Inc.; Maryland Financial Bank; First Capital Bancorp, Inc.; Tri-State Bank of Memphis; Fortune Financial Corporation; BancStar, Inc.; Titonka Bancshares, Inc; Millennium Bancorp, Inc.; TriSummit Bank; Prairie Star Bancshares, Inc.; Community First Bancshares, Inc.; BCB Holding Company, Inc.; City National Bancshares Corporation; First Business Bank, N.A.; SV Financial, Inc.; Capital Commerce Bancorp, Inc.; Metropolitan Capital Bancorp, Inc.; Bank of the Carolinas Corporation; Penn Liberty Financial Corp.; Tifton Banking Company; Patterson Bancshares, Inc; BNB Financial Services Corporation; Omega Capital Corp.; Mackinac Financial Corporation; Birmingham Bloomfield Bancshares, Inc; Vision

Charles McKay

Bank; Oregon Bancorp, Inc.; Peoples Bancorporation, Inc.; Indiana Bank Corp.; Business Bancshares, Inc.; Standard Bancshares, Inc.; York Traditions Bank; Grand Capital Corporation; Allied First Bancorp, Inc.; Frontier Bancshares, Inc.; Village Bank and Trust Financial Corp.; CenterBank; Georgia Primary Bank; Union Bank & Trust Company; HPK Financial Corporation; OSB Financial Services, Inc.; Security State Bank Holding-Company; Highlands State Bank; One Georgia Bank; Gateway Bancshares, Inc.; Freeport Bancshares, Inc.; Investors Financial Corporation of Pettis County, Inc.; Sword Financial Corporation; Premier Bancorp, Inc.; Mercantile Bank Corporation; Northern State Bank; Western Reserve Bancorp, Inc; Community Financial Shares, Inc.; Worthington Financial Holdings, Inc.; First Community Bancshares, Inc; Southern Heritage Bancshares, Inc.; Foresight Financial Group, Inc.; IBC Bancorp, Inc.; Boscobel Bancorp, Inc; Brogan Bankshares, Inc.; Riverside Bancshares, Inc.; Deerfield Financial Corporation; Market Street Bancshares, Inc.; The Landrum Company; First Advantage Bancshares, Inc.; Fort Lee Federal Savings Bank; Blackridge Financial, Inc.; Illinois State Bancorp, Inc.; Universal Bancorp; Franklin Bancorp, Inc.; Commonwealth Bancshares, Inc.; Premier Financial Corp; F & C Bancorp, Inc.; Diamond Bancorp, Inc.; United Bank Corporation; Community Bank Shares of Indiana, Inc.; American Premier Bancorp; CB Holding Corp.; Citizens Bancshares Co.; Grand Mountain Bancshares, Inc.; Two Rivers Financial Group; Fidelity Bancorp, Inc; Chambers Bancshares, Inc.; Covenant Financial Corporation; First Trust Corporation; OneFinancial Corporation;

Berkshire Bancorp, Inc.; First Vernon Bancshares, Inc.; SouthFirst Bancshares, Inc.; Virginia Company Bank; Enterprise Financial Services Group, Inc.; First Financial Bancshares, Inc.; River Valley Bancorporation, Inc.; Merchants and Manufacturers Bank Corporation; RCB Financial Corporation; Manhattan Bancshares, Inc.; Biscayne Bancshares, Inc.; Duke Financial Group, Inc.; Farmers Enterprises, Inc.; Century Financial Services Corporation; NEMO Bancshares, Inc.; University Financial Corp, Inc.; Suburban Illinois Bancorp, Inc.; Hartford Financial Services Group, Inc.; Fidelity Resources Company; Waukesha Bankshares, Inc.; FC Holdings, Inc.; Security Capital Corporation; First Alliance Bancshares, Inc.; Gulfstream Bancshares, Inc.; Gold Canyon Bank Gold; M&F Bancorp, Inc.; Metropolitan Bank Group, Inc.; NC Bancorp, Inc.; Alliance Bancshares, Inc.; Stearns Financial Services, Inc.; Signature Bancshares, Inc.; Fremont Bancorporation; Alliance Financial Services, Inc.; Lincoln National Corporation; Bancorp Financial, Inc.; Brotherhood Bancshares, Inc.; SouthCrest Financial Group, Inc.; Harbor Bankshares Corporation; First South Bancorp, Inc.; Great River Holding Company; Plato Holdings, Inc.; Yadkin Valley Financial Corp.; Community Bancshares, Inc.; Florida Bank Group, Inc.; First American Bank Corp.; Chicago Shore Corp.; Financial Services of Winger, Inc.; The ANB Corporation; U.S. Century Bank; Bank Financial Services, Inc.; KS Bancorp, Inc.; AmFirst Financial Services, Inc.; First Independence Corp.; First Guaranty Bancshares, Inc.; CoastalSouth Bancshares, Inc.; TCB Corporation; The State Bank of Bartley; Pathfinder Bancorp, Inc.;

Community Bancshares of Mississippi, Inc.; Heartland Bancshares, Inc.; PFSB Bancorporation, Inc.; First Eagle Bancshares, Inc.; IA Bancorp, Inc.; HomeTown Bankshares Corporation; Heritage Bankshares, Inc.; Mountain Valley Bancshares; Grand Financial Corp.; Guaranty Capital Corp.; GulfSouth Private Bank; Steele Street Bank Corp.; Premier Financial Bancorp; Providence Bank; Regents Bancshares; and Cardinal Bancorp II.

Over $200 billion dollars were given out, and $70 billion was paid back as of November 11, 2009.

New Strategies on Real Estate Investments in the Bailout Era

New Financial Deals in Commercial Real Estate

Institutions have started to sell leases on the secondary market. What's attractive is that these deals provide cash flow. Expenses are rolled up to the tenant, if it's in the contract. An example would be a $20,000,000 note with a coupon of 8 percent over twenty years. The tenant is responsible for maintenance, utilities, taxes, and insurance. These deals are being offered at 10 percent of the value. This type of deal provides an advantage over buying the property or the mortgage. The risk is whether the tenant will be around for the longer term.

Supermarkets are prime candidates for a securitized-lease deal. Supermarkets are large, stable tenants, and they seem to be for the most part recession-proof. The mortgage notes are available to investors. A deal like this can be risky if there are anomalies. Sub-leased properties provide such risks for many insurance companies. Balloon payments in sub-leased arrangements are uninsured. Consequently, since insurance companies stay away from these notes, financial institutions packaged the note's cash flows to be purchased by alternative interested buyers.

How Financing Has Changed in Commercial Real Estate since the Bank Bailout

Traditional commercial lending institutions have reviewed two areas. Up until the mortgage bailout crisis, it was mainly the property type and location that were considered during evaluation. Now, lenders are interested in knowing if there's a vacancy in the building. Also, lenders are interested in knowing if there's a lease coming up that has not been renewed. Not renewing the lease means that there's a strong potential for cash flow to decrease and hence a potential difference in the ability to meet the debt service requirements.

Since the mortgage bank bailout crisis, lenders have been more thorough. Lenders look more closely at the borrower. Borrowers have given building keys back to lenders and turned properties over when they were not able to make the property perform as expected. Traditional lenders want the borrower's net worth to be one to one with the amount being borrowed, or at most 87 percent of the net worth. Lenders take into account the borrower's other income sources.

Charles McKay

At the beginning of 2009, the market was slow in regards to buying debt. The market has been over-inflated on the debt side. Some brokers that sell debt feel as though the bailout has slowed the process down. One broker I'm friends with said, "Extend and pretend. Make sure the values are OK." This means extend the loan term and pretend things are fine. It is evident that people want the values that they were getting in 2005–06. Consequently, those properties purchased on the commercial side during those years are having problems. "The banks want to juice the price. It seems like the banks want more money and want people to juice things and get paid more money."

When determining values on the commercial side, there have been drops in apartment valuations because there is cheaper and alternative housing. There are vacancies on retail, which has been hit hard. Many store owners cannot make the rent, which forces the owner to re-work the leases instead of having the building go dark. If the property owner has the property over-leveraged, then the owner has to pay the bank mortgage using capital from other sources. Rents are in decline. It seems like office space is coming back at reduced pricing and the prices are fluctuating. In some geographic areas, re-working maturing loans on under-occupied buildings may be difficult. Hotels have been hurt the worst as a property type because people are not traveling and they are not using the lower-end hotels as much either. Some travelers are finding alternative places to stay and people cannot afford the higher-end services. Many hotels are over-leveraged. By and large, many brokers feel as though the government intervention is slowing down the pain for owners and investors.

Banks are dealing with commercial paper and do not want to write down the loss. At the moment, they're using their reserves. Many do not have enough money to cover the write-down and hope that the economy will turn around. The banks that are in trouble merge if possible. Banks are reluctant to sell their bad loans, and many owners are not paying their mortgages. Some owners pocket the rent money. Construction loans are getting pulled. Many tenants in retail have gone bankrupt and cannot pay their rent. In some areas of the country you have forty-unit condos that are half completed. In locations where construction loans are pulled by the bank, the real estate developer may have to go into bankruptcy to re-work loan obligations. Apartments in certain areas have cash flow and are good loans. Some banks are selling off the good loans so that they can build up cash. Most banks are not willing to write down the loan to the true value of the property.

It is a bit harder to purchase a property post-bailout, unless you are a first-time homebuyer. Soon, banks will probably identify properties that will default. Right now, borrowers have to either raise capital to cover the mortgage or extend the loan. Most banks do not want to take commercial properties back because they do not know how and do not want to manage the property.

On the other side, the market is easier for cash buyers. Cash buyers can get the property for the unpaid balance price, and the property is not discounted as much. An all-cash buyer just tells the bank that they want to take them out of the picture and gets the property. For entirely new acquisitions, a large number of banks are lending at a 65 percent loan to value (LTV) ratio, but the leverage could go to 50 percent LTV with more conservative lenders. Some government lenders will give 85 percent loan to value on apartment buildings. Insurance companies are lending on conservative deals.

Local banks are doing conventional loans. It's difficult to gauge, but the perception is that more banks received money from the treasury than what's advertised. Today, the banks can do fixed loans and borrow the money cheaply and get low interest loans from the government. It's a great deal to borrow money at around 25 basis points and then lend money at 4.5 percent interest. This enables the banks to build up their reserves.

Let's take a look at the flip side. What if the banks were to write down all of their losses at once, like what most businesses do? The losses would be great. Many banks would be insolvent and be upside down on the balance sheet. For that reason, with the bailout money, there are banks that use their reserves for operations. For their real estate assets, they are not being forced to mark down the value. The banks do not have to notify anyone what the current actual property value really is. A 20-million-dollar project a few years ago may be worth 4 million dollars today. The banks are not willing to write off the 16-million-dollar loss yet. The brokers that sold that project at that time received their fee at 20 million. The perception is that industrial land is worth less if no one is building on the property. Many owners do not want to pay the taxes associated with the property if they are not receiving any rent from the land. Some brokers that value property have the perception that banks that received bailout money are giving themselves the 20 to 30 percent bonuses that they've been used to over the years instead of writing down the bad debt. The bonuses have always been a part of the compensation system and how several banks have operated. If the bonuses go away, then the lifestyle that bankers have been accustomed to changes.

What kind of buffer do banks have today? Some have 130 percent buffer in reserve. If a buyer purchases debt that is not being paid on, it may take two years to get to court. In the meantime, someone has to maintain the property where the mortgage is not being paid. The cost of buying bad debt in the markets today can make matters worse for buyers if they do not have a team that is going to negotiate in every way with the sellers (who just want their fee).

Investment Options in Real Estate

Now, there are many investment options available associated with real estate. Which should you purchase: a mortgage, a securitized lease, or the actual property? There are many considerations before arriving at a decision. What kind of mortgage is on the property? Second, is the mortgage wrapped with other mortgages? Third, are there multiple properties involved? Multiple properties change the obligations of the borrower. The borrower cannot simply disregard one of the properties if the property is not performing. The borrower must pay for multiple properties under a single mortgage.

So the buyer must answer a few questions. As the buyer, are you able to make the property perform? Where's the risk on each available option? There are different tax considerations with each option. The most likely risks associated with a property are the deviation in operational costs, revenues from tenants, unexpected capital expenditures, and unexpected changes in taxes. When purchasing a securitized mortgage, the cash flow note is the most important. The stability and net worth of the owner are more important than any other aspect. With a securitized lease, there are little considerations when it comes to taxes. The main risk with securitized lease is the financial stability of the tenant.

Tax Credits

The tax credit program has done a few things for the real estate industry. Some items in the program are beneficial. This gets new "good" loans into the system that are supposed to perform for the banks and get cash into the banks reserves, which will ultimately pay back the amount that was received during the bailout process. What's broken is that the real estate agents, lenders, and appraisers work together to get the most money out of the borrower. Everyone still works for the seller, otherwise known as the listing agent. The appraiser secretly agrees with the listing agent and designated broker on the price, and the borrower looking to buy a new home is screwed. So what's changed? Not much. The borrower gets less for his or her money. The alliance between lender, real estate broker, appraiser, and broker opinion remains strong.

Tax credits from improving your home using approved green energy alternatives are also available for windows, doors, heating, insulation, cooling equipment, and heating systems. First, save your receipts and all associated paperwork. Alternative efficient energy, such as wind, solar, and geothermal, is at the forefront.

New Purchase Options

Today, some lenders have become creative when making it possible for an owner to purchase a new property. The lender refinances the current property and uses the difference towards the down payment of the new acquisition. The pros to this arrangement are obtaining a new property with no money down. There are drawbacks. This arrangement can potentially be toxic depending on the loan type and if there are dependencies with the mortgage tied by the lender. The result of this arrangement is a new bank loan number, a separate mortgage with a fixed rate, no balloon payments, and non-recourse.

Commercial Brokerage Thoughts on Bailout Process

Many commercial mortgage brokers want cash buyers to stay clear of bailout banks for fear that something odd may occur with the asset when the government is involved. The properties for sale by FDIC banks have been in spurts and have not been in the best shape, but they provide opportunity for those that know the community and that are willing to put money into the asset for resale.

Private Equity Post-bailout

Private equity firms have found areas where there's opportunity in the current climate. Some private equity firms continue to invest money into their existing, half-occupied assets while waiting for the market to turn around. Other firms in the acquisition phase are waiting for the targets to appear at the right price given their firms' strategies.

My Real Estate Portfolio Is Not Performing, Now What?

If your loans are not performing, then as a private equity firm or a bailout bank you have a few options. Change your policies, sell your assets, change management, or hold on and wait. Holding onto assets has not worked too well for publicly traded companies. Revenue forecasts have been missed and more funds have been needed, just to preserve jobs.

Bank Bailout Impact

The bailout on the banks represents different things to people. Taxpayer money has been used to add to the cash reserves of the banks. If the banks have not paid the money back yet, then the money from the treasury is being used to fund operations. Managers and executives have had their salaries capped in many cases. Do you think that capping salaries is fair? To some executives it is not fair. So what about the flip side? Cash deposits from customers were used to purchase mortgage-backed securities, collateralized debt, and loan obligations that did not get their return on investment. In the majority of instances, the bulk of them have had trouble being valued and are considered worthless by some professionals in the field today. So should executives be rewarded for making sweeping mistakes? Many have been salary capped at a $500,000 salary. Some argue that many of these executives will leave for other firms if they cannot continue to receive the paychecks that support their lifestyles. Sometimes it's better to allow them to leave to determine their true value and to recruit new leadership. Salaries, promotions, and bonuses are negotiable by the government for banks that are not in a position to pay back bailout money and that continue to underperform. Perhaps long-term equity and bonuses paid on a three- to five-year performance streak should be the new standard for bank executives bound to the TARP.

Over $500 billion have been spent in the TARP with $200 billion going to specific firms. The management teams at banks should be more responsible for making banks perform without the aid of the federal government by making smarter decisions. It's estimated that Citibank and Bank of America have each received over $40 billion. It's estimated that AIG has received over $60 billion. The assets were not as much as their books claimed, and many creditors still have not taken their losses. Both Federal Reserve debt and TARP dollars must be repaid.

It's smart if housing prices are not boosted by appraisers. If the appraisers do not boost the price, then those that insure these properties will not lose their shirts if there's another catastrophe. FHA, Federal Housing Authority, is one such entity.

What does the United States do with unused TARP money or money that's been paid back? Should money go to homeowners who have lost their jobs to keep them in their homes? This would depend both on the circumstance and what the government is willing to do to be in a position of re-election. If a family was sold a home during the housing bubble and if it's not worth nearly as much today, then why not correct the mistake that the real estate brokers, banks, and appraisers made and help keep the homeowner in the house by temporarily or permanently supplementing the payment? What's the alternative? Keep the bad loan, foreclose, and have toxic assets in the neighborhood. Should your bank get bailed out or closed down? I believe that it depends on the circumstances. If the bailout is primarily due to the mistakes on loaning out money on properties that were improperly valued during the real estate bubble, then perhaps these banks need temporary assistance and advice on a future direction. If the bailout is due to underperforming business loans, then change bank management and policy. Unused bailout money should also commit to sourcing jobs through a new federal administrative program to entrepreneurs developing new, innovate businesses.

Smart Real Estate Deals in the Bank Bailout Era and Beyond

When banks fail, getting credit and loans becomes more difficult. This makes the process more difficult for people looking to buy cars, homes, and property and perhaps for student trying to obtain educational loans. Money for loans also tightens for businesses that need to fulfill payroll obligations.

Lowering interest rates across the board enables everyone to save money and take advantage and save money across the board. What happens when the government reduces the cost of mortgage payments to 31 percent? If the real estate brokers do not get into responding by convincing the appraisers and broker price opinions to increase the value, then it saves homeowners a lot of money. If the appraisers and brokers in particular markets get together secretly and decide that they want to tell everyone that the prices are going to go up, then we are potentially right back into a vicious cycle that we were in previously in 2004–06, when everything started getting marked up and the brokers wanted extra money for their fees.

Part Four:
In Trouble with Your Mortgage

If you're facing foreclosure and have no other options to cover your debt owed to the bank, consider a short sale over foreclosing.

Foreclosure versus Short Sale

If an owner is unable to refinance their property after exhausting several lenders and raising money from family and friends, then the owner should consider a short sale of the property to avoid official foreclosure. There are homeowner consequences when considering each in the areas of credit score, credit history, current employment, future employment, deficiency judgment, and deficiency amount.

Credit Score Issue

Your score is lowered to 250–300 if there's a foreclosure. The credit score is influenced for three years. During a short sale, only late payments show up. After the sale, the mortgage will confirm as being paid or negotiated. The short sale can lower your score by fifty points.

Credit History

A foreclosure will remain on a person's credit history for ten years.

Current Employment

Short sales are not reported on your credit. If an employee handles sensitive information, then an employer may verify his or her credit often. A foreclosure can influence termination or reassignment to another position.

Future Employment

Employers may require a credit check. A foreclosure can confront employment. A short sale is not reported on your credit record and therefore does not oppose employment.

Deficiency Judgment

During foreclosure, the bank has the right to pursue deficiency judgment. With a short sale, it's feasible to get the bank to give up the right to deficiency judgment against the homeowner.

Deficiency Amount

During foreclosure, if the property does not sell at auction, then the sales price is lowered. During a short sale, the property is sold very close to market value. The short sale is superior to the REO sale, resulting in lower deficiency.

Part Five:
Going Pro as a Real Estate Professional

Those that wish to make real estate a part of their profession may find these real estate best practices for salespeople, portfolio management roles, and investment objectives useful in their career pursuit.

Real Estate Sales Best Practices

For people that are selling and marketing property, start and maintain best practices. First, stay current on sales trends. Next, enroll in classes and perfect your sales pitch. Second, great salespeople always pursue leads and prospects. Establishing relationships with leads and prospects can generate sales referrals. Third, position yourself and join trade organizations. Market what you do and let people know where you can add value. Fourth, do not live in front of the computer. Arrange face-to-face meetings with the prospects. Fifth, qualify the buyer and determine who has the authority to spend.

Charles McKay

Positions in Portfolio Management

For portfolio investment real estate, the endowment manager, the investment manager, the operating partner, and the property manager must work as a unit to increase the cash flows and value of the asset. The endowment manager concentrates on strategy. The investment manager unifies portfolio management. The operating partner is responsible for financing and asset management. The property manager maintains the upkeep of the property.

The endowment manager decides where the money will be allocated and creates a plan sponsor strategy. Sourcing, underwriting, and establishing investment partnerships are the focus of the tasks.

The investment manager selects the type of real estate product and geographic allocation of the properties. He or she formulates the real estate portfolio strategy and tactics. In addition, the manager obtains the funds for transactions, negotiates and formulates partnership joint ventures, and secures financing for debt and equity. Investment managers also determine the exit strategy. They controls major capital and asset decisions and report on the performance.

The operating partner discovers property opportunities, determines the strategy and creates the business plan. He or she executes the operational plan including acquisition, leasing, development, financing, and sales.

The property manager sets goals and budgeting and performs accounting and financial reporting. The property manager administers the lease and performs billing and collections, procurement, maintenance, tax, and capital improvements. He or she maintains and improves relationships with tenants.

Real Estate Portfolio Investment Objectives

When building a real estate portfolio it's important to provide immediate income, to diversify asset holdings, and to protect against inflation.

Liquidity, taxes, property management cost, and time horizon are critical factors when investing. In the investment approach, the investor may be inclined to provide value add services that may be more expensive and outperform the market, follow market trends, or have an opportunistic approach. Domestic and cross-border investments differ in risk, return, yield, and spread.

Investment managers may desire to add value and mitigate risk through real estate diversification in industrial, retail, office, hotel, and apartments. Each product type has different demands. Market approach may vary in growth, stability, value, and cost.

Investment managers should study the market, the size of the product, the political climate, and financial goals. The manager is compelled to produce a cohesive risk and return analysis for each investment stage. Safeguards ensure that exposure is not exceeded. Deal and financial structure directly influence investment cash flow and returns.

Part Six:
Smart Real Estate Deals

By now, it's obvious that the traditional process of valuing real estate is broken and is not in the best interest of the investor, buyer, banks, and Wall Street investors. It's now time to make smart real estate deals. Leverage for Real Estate Investment Personal Edition is an invention that I made to help homeowners, investors, lenders, accountants, real estate professionals, and bailout banks who've got themselves into trouble find their way out of the woods. I have three additional inventions to help, but this one should help most readers save money immediately. Please read the tutorial to make smarter deals. A specific real estate investment scenario ends this section.

Tutorial Overview of Leverage for Real Estate Investment

Download **Leverage 4.0 (Personal Edition)** from *www.glacierconcept.com*. Email sales@glacierconcept.com

Charles McKay

From the start page, press the Forecast button on the upper left corner.

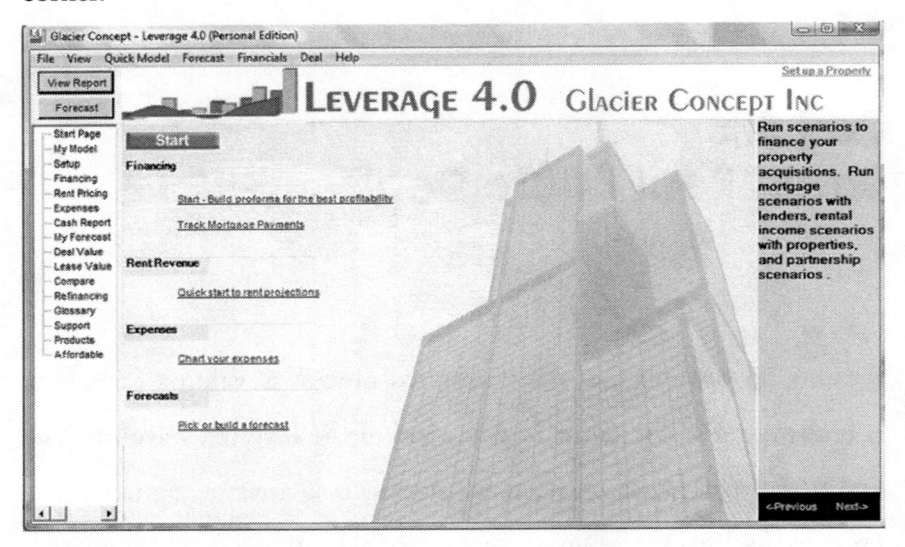

From the splash screen, you can start your mortgage financing, make rent projections, fill out a template for operational expenses, or go directly to forecasts. Use the "Previous" and "Next" buttons from this window to get tips on how to use the software. The left-hand-pane navigation system allows you easily to determine an affordable mortgage, determine how much money you will save from a refinancing scenario, determine the value of leases, determine an affordable property based on your income, or create a scenario step by step to generate a pro forma report and charts for investors.

To determine an affordable mortgage and your affordable property, select the "Affordable" link in the left-hand-pane navigation area. By entering your gross annual income, the loan to value bank terms, interest rate, and mortgage term years, the resulting affordable mortgage and affordable property will be shown in the result. Use the window as a baseline for negotiation and do not let the property sellers convince you as a buyer to deviate too much from this amount.

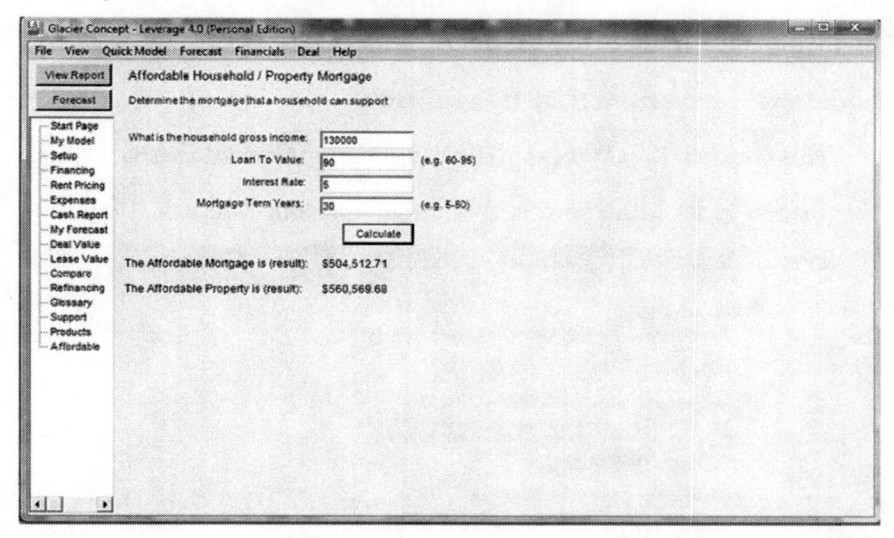

From the forecast menu, choose: build a forecast, build a high-level forecast, open an existing forecast, copy a forecast from a saved pro forma, or go to Leverage 4.0 online. To return here, select **My Forecast** from the left-hand pane.

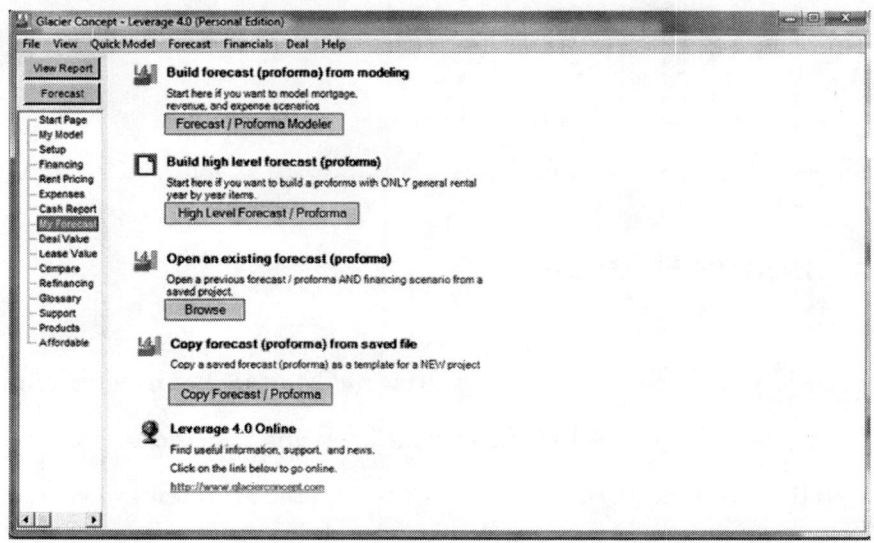

If you choose to build a forecast, you can build a real estate financial model step —by step. Follow all the steps to build your scenario and financing model. Select **My Model** to return to the window at any point in the application from the left-hand pane.

This window takes you step —by step without spread sheets through the process of building your real estate investment forecast.

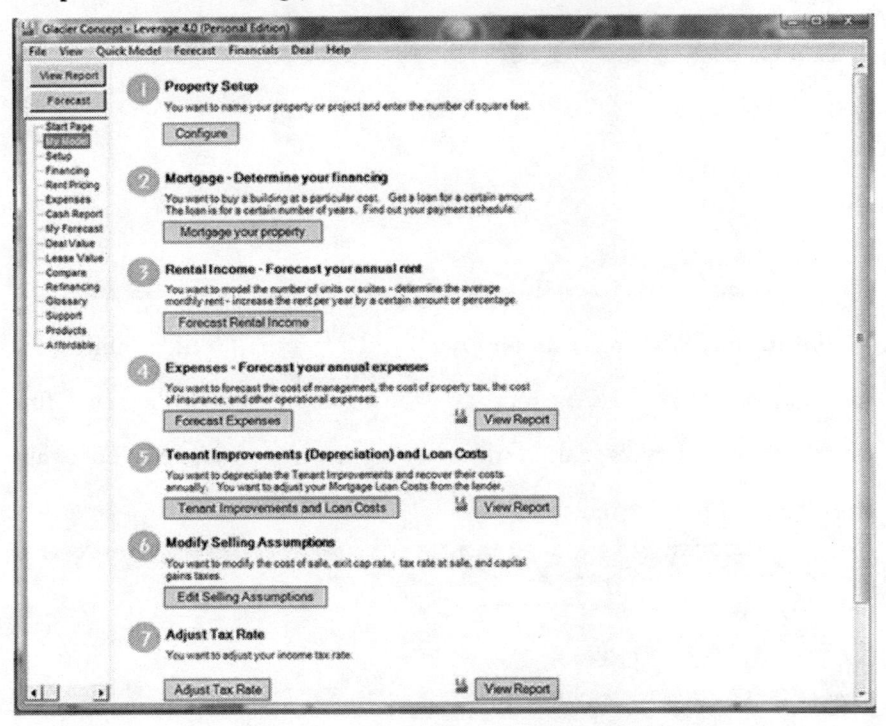

Mortgage Financing

Finance your property. You must press the **Map-to-Loan** button for your data to be mapped to the current financing scenario to preserve your data. You must also 'Save' your data from the **File menu** when you

Smart Real Estate Deals in the Bank Bailout Era and Beyond

finish your model to refer to it later again and work on your file later. You may want to choose the 'sensitivity' button to see how mortgage interest (bank profit) and monthly payments will vary with interest rates and number of years of your mortgage. This helps fully analyze what you will have to pay back and what you will be saving in the long term.

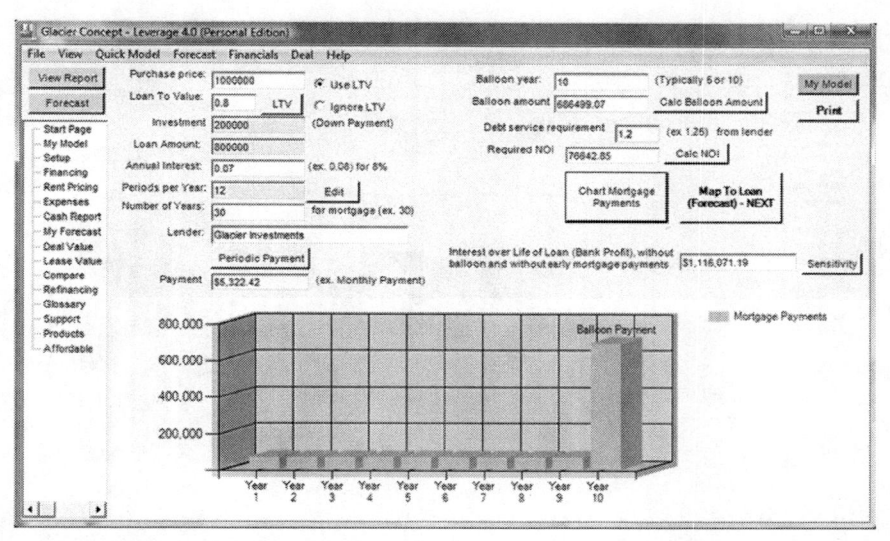

Homeowners, investors, and lenders make the most of this window by coming up with loan terms and saving the terms on the **File menu**. The user presses the sensitivity button to view finance options based on interest rate sensitivity analysis to facilitate saving money.

Rent projections

You can project your rent and see the results visually before deciding to preserve the information. Change the numbers as much as you want and select the "Make Projection" button, until you are satisfied. When you select **Map to Proforma**, the rental income numbers are preserved in the model. Map to Proforma will take you to the view report screen and allow you to see your projections results reflected in the report. If you want to save your information to a file, you must select **Save As** from the **File menu**. Your effective rental income is determined from your projection results in the chart.

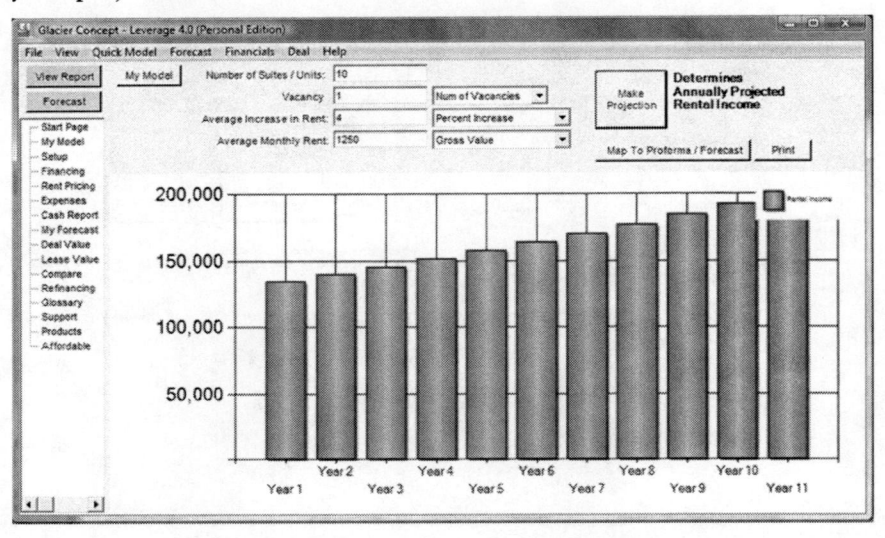

You can adjust the rent projections on the fly and use a number of different rent metrics from gross value to per square foot. Using a market value per square foot should be reasonable to start, unless you believe that a premium rent rate can realistically be obtained. Print out the rent projection forecast to make a presentation or to show other investors.

Expenses (Individual)

Project individual expenses. Management expense fees are typically part of rental income and range from 3 to 8 percent. **Enter 0.03 for 3 percent.** You can also derive your expenses from an ad-hoc rental income, if you have not previously generated your rent projections. Property taxes, insurance, maintenance, and other expenses may be entered in **gross value, percentage rent, or per square foot**. Select the appropriate option from the drop-down list. If you want to enter **5 cents per square foot**, you must enter it as **0.05**. Your individual expenses will be charted, and the first year overall expenses will appear in the **first year total expenses** field. Select **map to proforma** to preserve your information in your model.

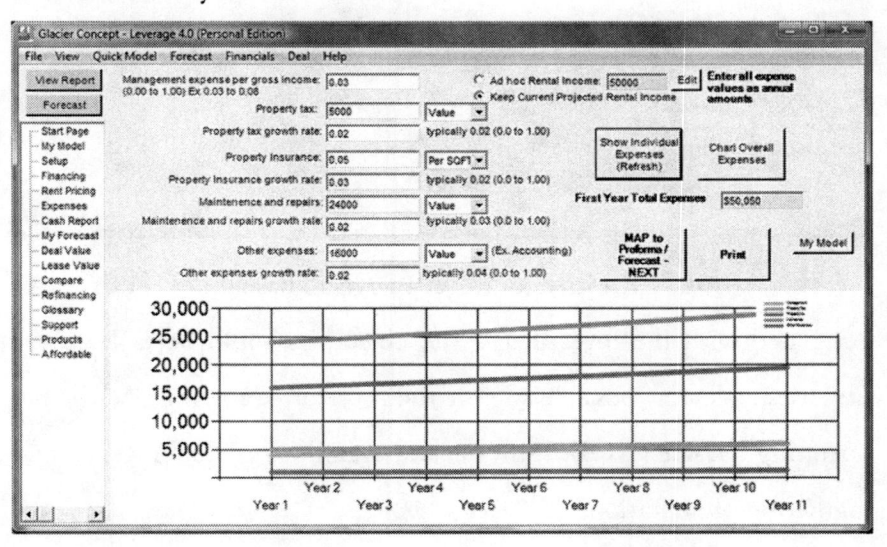

Annual accounting fees, HVAC, or heating costs can be estimated and projected in the "other expenses" text field. Print out the individual expenses to make a presentation.

Expenses (Overall)

To view your overall expenses, select the Chart Overall expenses button.

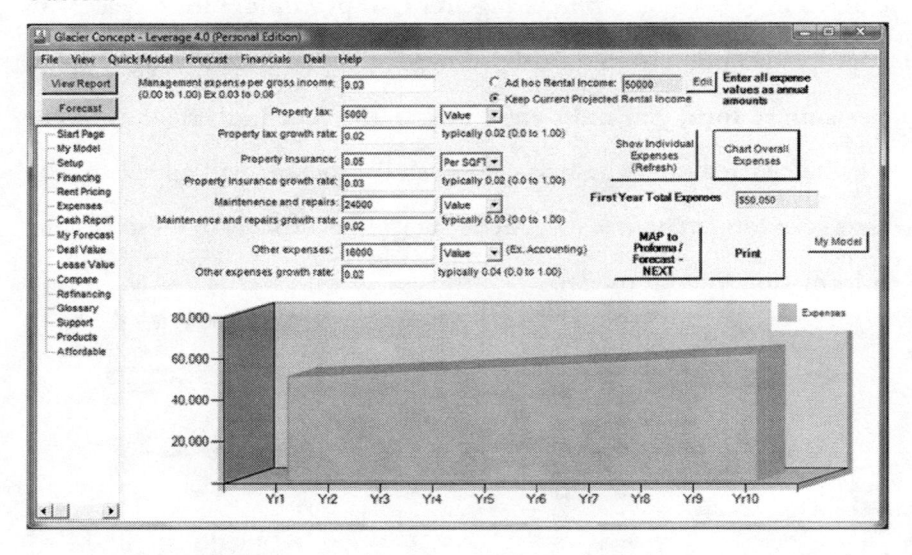

This is used for the investor to get an overall baseline of the expenses associated with the investment. The objective should be to keep the expenses as low as possible so that the investor can maximize the net operating income (NOI). Print out the overall expenses for a sales and marketing presentation.

Property Setup and Configuration

Configure your property name and square footage. When you are done, apply your changes (**Apply Changes**) and select the **Next** button. You will return to the **My Model** window.

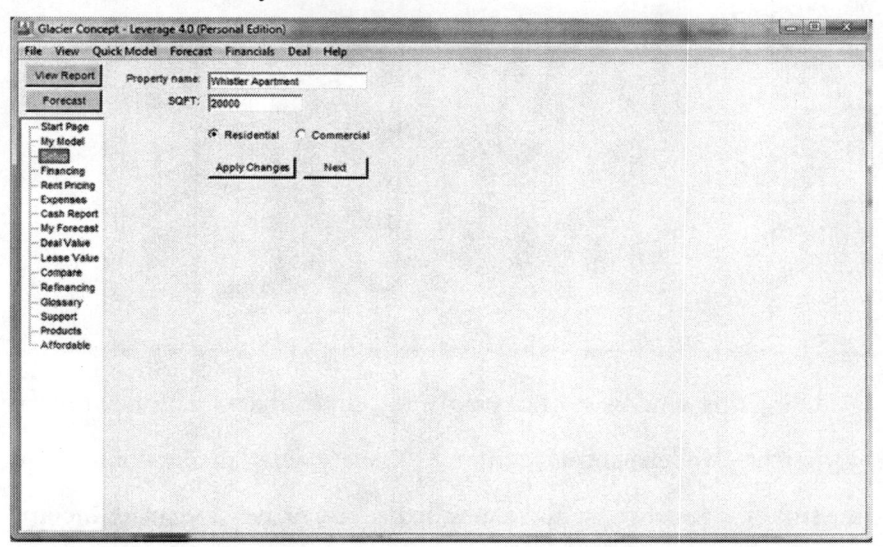

Enter the project or property name that you are evaluating on this window. You can specify the number of square feet and enter whether the property is commercial or residential. There are accounting differences in residential and commercial properties. Please select the appropriate radio button and press the "Apply Changes" button.

Financial Review

Finally, go to the financial review window to chart the revenue, expenses, and NOI (net operating income). You can also print any one of these individually for a presentation. This gives you an overview of your projected outcome.

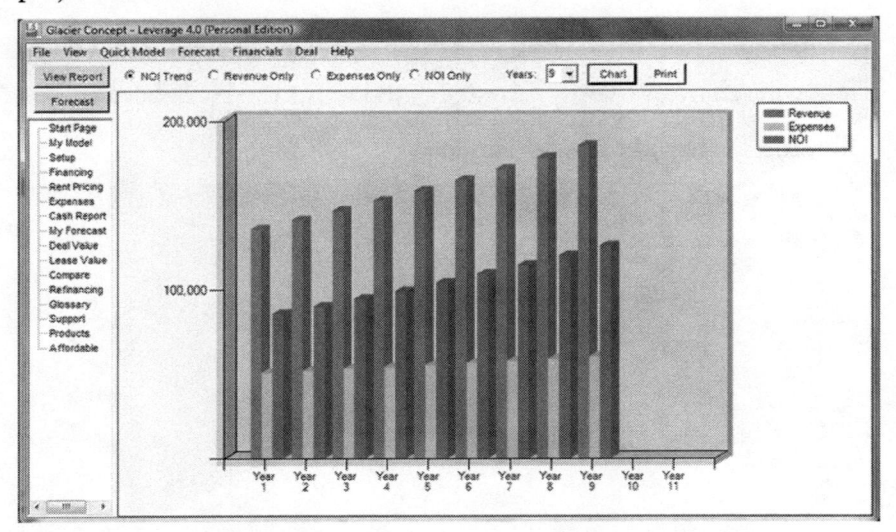

Using this window to print graphs and charts that will be meaningful to investors, lenders, and accountants in determining the feasibility of an investment opportunity. Revenues, expenses, or net operating income can be individually charted and printed out using this window.

Report Output

View the results in the report. This may be accessed at any time by selecting the View Report button on the top left of Leverage 4.0 Personal Edition. You may also review numbers graphically and print them out in the bottom pane.

Smart Real Estate Deals in the Bank Bailout Era and Beyond

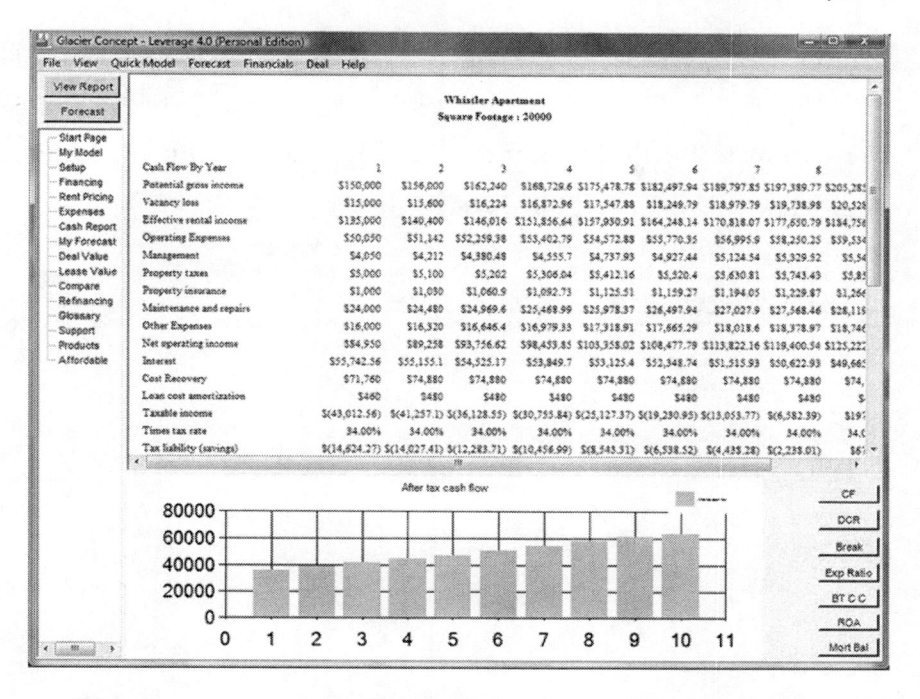

[Screenshot of Glacier Concept - Leverage 4.0 (Personal Edition) software showing Whistler Apartment cash flow report with 8-year projection and After tax cash flow bar chart]

This report is part of the detailed output of the financial model pro forma. Accountants and banks typically would like to review this information. The chart in the bottom pane shows the change in mortgage balance, cash flows, debt service coverage, and other performance-related ratios that most people in finance evaluate. Any one of these metrics can be printed out. After this report is fully populated you can view the internal rate of return from the menu.

Lease Value

Find out how much money your lease is worth if you have someone sign a contract today worth a certain number of dollars. This helps you understand the impact of having a person sign a lease today for a certain number of years. You can also get to this window from the **Lease Value** in the left-hand pane. Note: Some windows may be disabled until you have paid for the application and contacted support (support@glacierconcept.com) to enable these features.

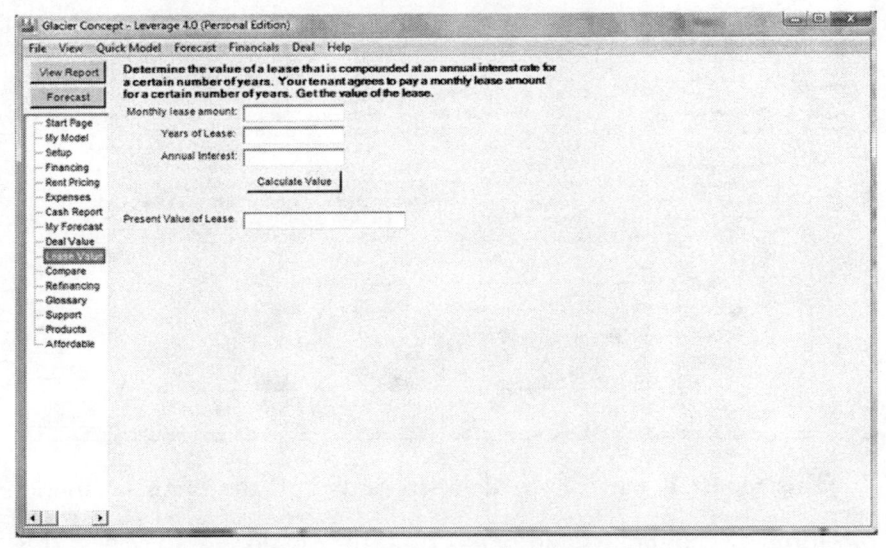

The lease may have an interest rate assigned. This will allow you to assign a simple lease contract that will grow with or greater than the inflation rate. Smart landlords will use this window for multiple-year lease contracts for prospective tenants.

Deal Value

Follow steps 1 and 2 before you sell the property. Then follow steps 1 and 2 after you sell the property to see where you maximize your return and when you make the most money. **Hint:** you may want to sell the property before your balloon payment is due. Otherwise, you can refinance when your balloon payment is due.

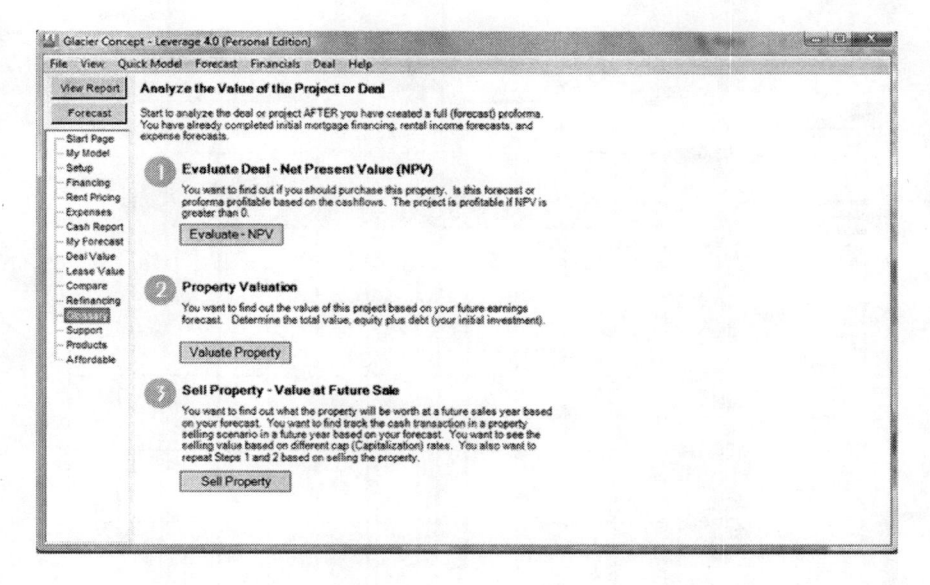

Evaluate Deal—Net Present Value (NPV)

Enter your target discount rate or **hurdle rate**. Evaluate the deal for a certain number of years. See the output and results. If NPV is greater than or equal to 0, this is a safe or good investment. The investment will be profitable in the year (**number of years**) that NPV is 0 or greater. Depending on your model, you may have to sell the property to make your money back and become profitable. In that case, you will have to select **Sell Property** and then conduct an NPV analysis.

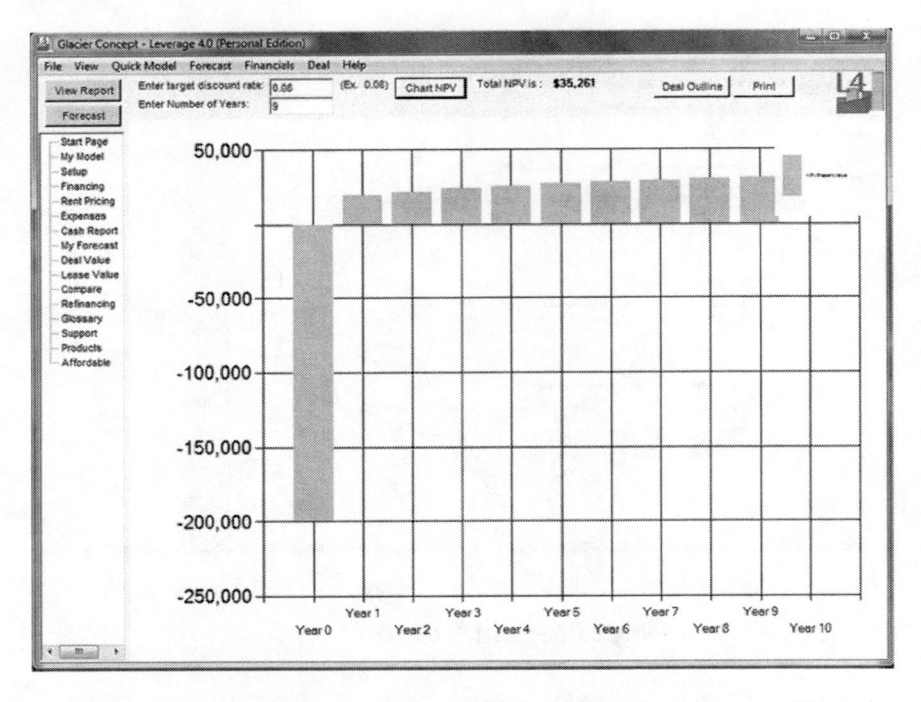

This window will let you know approximately when you'll make your money back and let you know whether you need to sell the property to make a profit, based on the financial model.

Property Valuation

Determine the value of your property. Enter the **target discount rate** or hurdle rate and the **number of years** that you want to use when valuing the property based on your model. If you do not select mortgage debt, you are conducting an equity-only valuation. If you select **include mortgage debt**, that is a **total valuation** without selling the property in the **number of years**. If you have conducted a scenario to "Sell the Property," you can select **Include Sale of Property**. This will let you know the total valuation of the deal when you choose to sell the property at a future date. The sale of the property typically takes place before your **balloon payment** is due on your loan. Your other options is to refinance instead of selling the property.

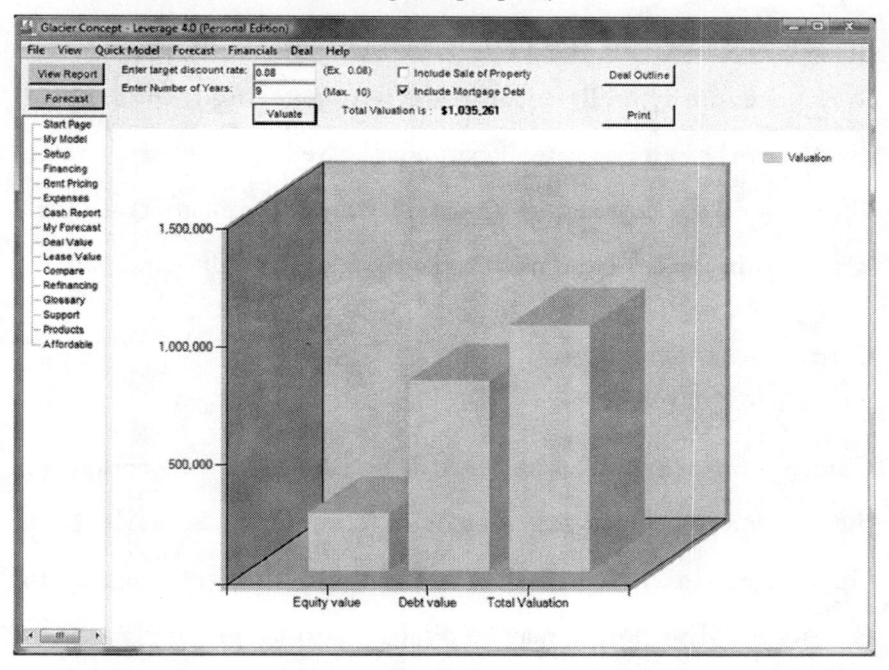

This will help you know whether the property is actually worth the broker's listing price and what your real expectations should be regarding investing in this property that you are evaluating. If the valuation is less than the broker's listing price, then the listing price is too high, given this financing and equity scenario. If that is the case, negotiate with the broker and offer a price more equivalent with the total valuation.

Sell Property—Value at Future date.

Select the year that you want to sell the property. Enter the market **exit cap rate** (Capitalization rate). The cap rate will vary from market to market. You may **edit and update** your changes to the cap rate here. Sales prices are typically equal to the **net operating income (NOI)** divided by the **exit cap rate**. Next press the **Sell the Property** button. The output is the entire sales transaction, before tax and after tax. There is a report in the left-hand pane and a chart in the right-hand pane.

Compare mortgages

Compare financing scenarios back to back to see which options are the best for you. Open scenarios by selecting **Open Scenario 1** and **Open Scenario 2.** Next, select the **Compare Mortgages** button for your results. This feature may be disabled until you have purchased a license. Contact support (support@glacierconcept.com) when you have purchased Leverage to enable this feature.

	Lincoln Place 24000 Sqft	Washington Square 20000 Sqft	Variance	Variance %
Lender	Silvermark Trust Bank	Waldenworth Bank		
Term	30	30	0	
Interest on Loan	618050.34	868786.42	250736.08	28.86
Loan Amount	750000	750000	0	
Periodic Payment	3800.14	4496.63	696.49	15.49
Lender Loan Costs	11250	11250	0	
Debt Service	45601.68	53959.55	8357.87	15.49
DSCR Required	1.5	1.2	-0.3	-25
Interest Rate	0.045	0.06	0.015	25

Investors can use this window to negotiate loan terms. Lenders can use this window to show potential customers how much money they will save if the use their services over another lender or mortgage broker.

Refinancing

Determine the amount saved by refinancing your property. You may want to refinance, even if you are not in a financial crunch. **Effective borrowing rate** is a rate that is slightly above your **new interest rate**, but below the **interest rate on original loan**. **Number of years to hold property before selling**—do you want to refinance if you plan on selling the property in, say, six years? Enter all your information on this screen and press the **'Refinance results'** button. Get to this window by pressing **Refinancing** in the left-hand pane.

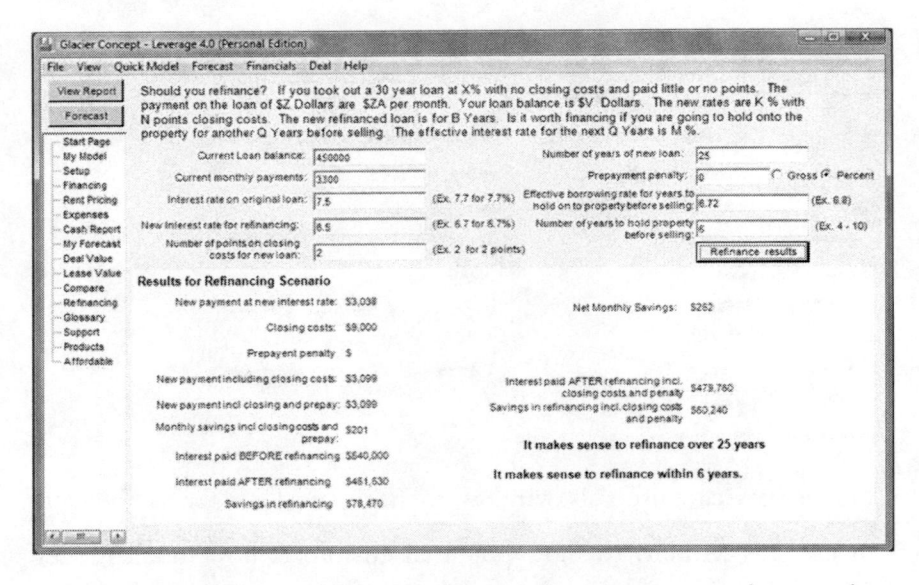

Investors and homeowners, this window gives you a bottom line of how much money you'll save over the course of the new loan and whether it makes sense to refinance given your assumptions. If you refinance in time, you can potentially prevent bank loan foreclosures. Lenders can use this window to convince homeowners to use their service in a loan modification scenario.

Customer Support

Contact support for help and enabling any windows after Leverage 4.0 has been purchased. Email support@glacierconcept.com.

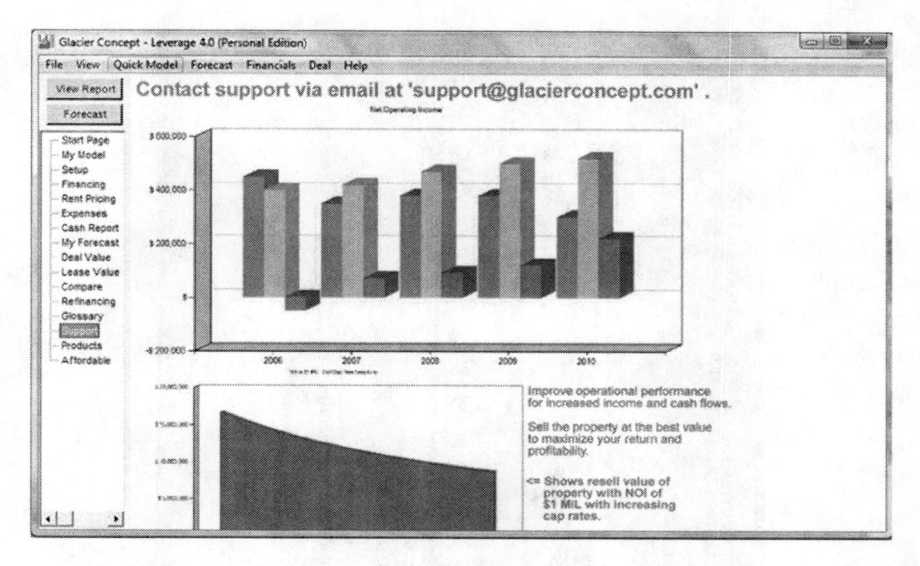

The affairs surrounding the improper valuation of real estate, negligent mortgage origination, exuberance, and the bank bailout makes my invention Leverage For Real Estate a great option for homeowners and investors to save time, save money, and make more intelligent real estate investment forecasting decisions.

Charles McKay

Getting Started: Real Estate Forecast—Leverage

To make smarter deals easy and fast, use Leverage for Real Estate Investment Personal Edition by Glacier Concept. Get the software download from *www.glacierconcept.com*.

When you start Leverage 4.0, click on "Forecast" in the upper left of the window. You may:

- Build a high-level pro forma or forecast

- Build a forecast or pro forma from modeling
- Open an existing pro forma or model
- Copy a pro forma from a saved file
- Go to the glacierconcept.com Web site for updates and news.

To get started quickly, select "Build pro forma from modeling."

- In a step-by-step process, perform the steps shown: mortgage, rental income, expenses, tenant improvements / loan costs, selling assumptions, adjusting tax rate, property setup, and review financials.

Review the performance of your model in any step by selecting the "view report" button.

Leverage 4.0 Usage Scenarios

1. You want to buy a building for $1,000,000

Open Leverage.

Click on Track Mortgage Payments from the 'Start Page'.

In the 'purchase price field', click on the 'use ltv' (Loan to Value) button.

In the purchase price field, enter '1000000' for $1,000,000.

Obtain a loan-to-value ratio from the lender at a bank or mortgage company. A good loan to value is either 0.8 or 0.9. In this example, enter '0.8', which represents an 80 percent loan to value.

Click on the 'LTV' button.

The Investment amount of $200,000 is required as a down payment.

The Loan Amount from the bank is $800,000.

Enter the annual interest. Either use 0.07 for 7 percent or 0.08 for 8 percent or ask the lender what the interest rate will be. Important Note: Ask the bank for a 'fixed interest rate,' not a floating or variable interest rate.

Enter the number of years for the mortgage. For a thirty-year loan, enter '30'.

> Press the 'Periodic payment' button to get your monthly payment.

In this example the result is $5870.12 as a periodic payment. You may have a balloon payment loan that performs a like a thirty-year loan up until the balloon year. In this case, if the balloon year is a ten-year balloon, enter '10' in the 'Balloon year' field.

> Press the 'Balloon amount' button, and the software shows you that $701,797.63 balloon payment is due at the end of year 10.

The lender will give you a debt service requirement or a debt service performance criteria. It will always have a value greater than 1 and may be up to or above 2. Enter the debt service requirement. In this example, enter '1.3' in the 'debt service requirement field'.

> The resulting Net Operating Income is $91,573.82 per year to meet the debt service needs of the bank.

Click 'Chart Mortgage Payments' to see the annual mortgage payments.

This enables the 'Map to Loan' button that allows you to map the mortgage financing scenario if you like it.

You may repeat any of the above steps for a different mortgage-financing scenario.

Rental Income Window

> This window allows the user to project (forecast) the rental income for ten to eleven years. The forecast in the chart is the projection.

Enter number of suits or units

- Eight-unit building
- Vacancy—can be either in percent vacant or number of vacancies (e.g., enter '11' for 11 percent and also select the 'percent vacant' in the combo-box, or you can set the number of average vacancies by selecting 'number of vacancies' in the combo-box and entering '1' or '2' in the edit field.)
- Average Increase in Rent—can be set to 'percent increase', 'dollar amount increase', or 'per square foot increase'. Per square foot increase can be used if you are charging rent of $15 per square foot and you want to increase the rent by $1 per square foot each year; in this case, you enter '1'and select 'per square foot increase'.
- Average Monthly Rent—enter full amount as either 'gross value', or 'per sqft (square foot)'. Gross value would be rent of, say, $1000 per month. Per square foot would be '$2 per square foot' on a 500-square-foot space or building.

Make projection

- Graphically charts the projected rent. If you are satisfied with the projection, click 'map to pro forma' to keep the numbers as the forecast. If you are not satisfied with the projection / forecast, change the numbers in the above fields and continue clicking the 'make projection' button until you are satisfied, and then select 'map to pro forma'.

Loan Costs

- Loan costs are charges by the lender to process the mortgage loan. The loan cost is a percentage that can be negotiated with the lender and will vary from lender to lender and on the total cost of the loan. The loan cost is an additional profit of the lender.
- Loan costs can be amortized over an amortization period; loan costs influence the cash flow calculation.

Selling Assumptions

- Are applied at the sale of the property. The sale of a property is also known as a capital event.
- Selling costs, Cap (capitalization) rate, tax rate at sale, and capital gains tax are applied in determining the before- and after-tax calculation of the property sale.
- The capital event is applied to the cash flow calculation in the year of the sale.

Adjust Tax Rate

- Allows adjustment of the income tax rate applied to the annual cash flow calculations for non-capital events.

Property Setup

- Allows the user to name the project for the financing and cash flow scenario. Allows the user to enter the total square footage of the property.
- The square footage (number of square feet) is applied to all per-square-foot calculations.

Review Financials

- Review financials window allows a user to create either an individual or a combined chart for revenues, operating expenses, or net operating income.
- The financials may be charted for a certain number of years as selected from the drop-down list.

Rate of Return (Internal Rate of Return) IRR

- The internal rate of return can be calculated before tax and after tax based on the cash flows on each.
- Tax liability is subtracted from the before-tax cash flow to obtain the after-tax cash flow. If the tax liability is negative, then the after-tax cash flow can be greater than the before-tax cash flow.

Analyze the real estate project or proposed deal

- Deals are proposed by brokers. Is the listing price of the property a fair deal? How profitable is this proposed deal based on the model that has been created? When will I make back the money that I invested? Deal analysis is done after the mortgage financing and both the rental income and expenses have been forecasted.

Evaluate Deal (NPV) Net Present Value analysis

- Conduct an NPV analysis to determine whether you should purchase a property. The project or deal is profitable if the NPV is greater than zero.
- A hurdle rate or discount rate is the amount/rate/percentage or minimum amount of return to make the deal worthwhile.
- The number of years will show the NPV calculation for the number of years that are being evaluated. The deal will be good in the year where NPV is at least zero.

Property Valuation

- Allows the user to find out the value of the property based on future earnings. The broker lists the property at a particular price. Is the property worth that amount based on the cash flow model that has been created? In what year will the property be worth that value based on the cash equity earned? What is the overall value of the property based on the cash model and a future sale of the property? This helps to gauge whether the property value is realistic, overvalued, or undervalued and distressed based on the cash flow model that has been created.
- Property value at a particular year is equal to the debt (initial investment) plus equity earned.

- Equity value will include the equity from cash flows, which may optionally include the sale of the property at some future date.
- The discount rate (hurdle rate) and number of years in the forecast to perform a valuation are input to determine the property value based on the model.

Selling Property

- The property may be sold in a future year. The initial offering sales price is typically the net operating income divided by the capitalization rate. Cap rates vary from market to market and may be modified in the model on the Selling property window.
- The output shows the sales price as a function of the capitalization rate in the year selected for the property sale.
- The Sell property button initiates a sales transaction.

Sales Transaction window

- Appears after the sell property window.
- Before tax—Displays the sale price, cost of sale, adjusted basis, total gain, total cost recovery taken, capital gain, and unamortized loan costs.
- After tax—displays the sale price, less cost of sale, less mortgage balance, sale proceeds before tax, tax on cost recovery recapture, tax on capital gain, tax loss on ordinary income, and sales proceeds after tax.

Lease Value

- Determines in today's dollars the cost of a lease (value of a lease) signed by a tenant based on the monthly lease amount, years of the lease, and the annual interest.
- In this scenario, your tenant agrees to pay a certain amount of money for rent monthly for a certain number of years. Determines the value of the lease.

Refinance

- Should you refinance your property? How should you negotiate the interest terms of your property?
- How much money can you save from refinancing your property? Should you refinance your property if you plan to sell the property within a certain number of years?
- Loan balance—your current loan balance. Monthly payment—your current monthly payment. Interest rate on the current loan. Number of years on the new loan—the number of years that the lender says that it will take to pay back the loan based on the lender's loan terms. New interest rate for refinancing the lender's rate for the refinanced loan (be careful here: negotiate a *fixed* annual interest rate. You can lose your property on annual percentage rate loans. Keep contacting lenders until you find one that will accept a fixed-rate mortgage).
- Number of points on closing costs—typically two or more points.

Smart Real Estate Deals in the Bank Bailout Era and Beyond

- Effective borrowing rate for years before selling property. This rate is an ad hoc rate that is slightly above the refinance rate but below the current loan rate. It serves as a hurdle rate or discount rate. Number of years to hold onto property before conducting a sales transaction on the property or a capital event.
- The Results window will evaluate your loan assumptions and your proposed timing on when you will sell the property in the not-so-distant future and let you know how much money you'll save over the life of the loan if you refinance, as well as if it's worth it to refinance even if you intend on selling the property in the near future.

Mortgage comparison

- Compares mortgage finance scenarios side by side. May or may not be for the same property. May or may not be from the same lender. Mortgage comparison helps determine and better negotiate better financing options among several lenders.
- Compare the interest amounts on loans (i.e., profit to the bank). Loan amounts, monthly payments, lender profits in loan costs, debt service requirements, and interest rates from lenders.
- Determine the better mortgage deal. Always negotiate fixed-rate debt.

Mortgage Sensitivity Analysis

- Allows user to modify the interest rate based on the current loan amount.

- Shows both the monthly payment and interest paid for the following loan years: 15, 20, 25, 30, and 50.
- Modify the interest rate and immediately see the impact on the monthly payments and the overall interest paid.